Practice*Planner*

Arthur E. Jongsma, Jr., Series Editor

Helping therapists help their clients...

Over 250,000 Practice*Planners* sold . . .

WILEY

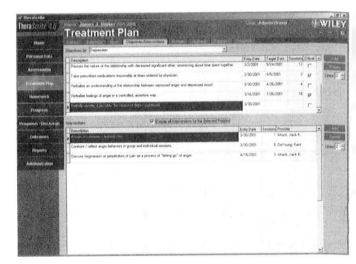

Practice *Planners*

Treatment Planners cover all the necessary elements for developing formal treatment plans, including detailed problem definitions, long-term goals, short-term objectives, therapeutic interventions, and DSM-IV™ diagnoses.

❏ **The Complete Adult Psychotherapy Treatment Planner,** Second Edition
0-471-31924-4 / $44.95

❏ **The Child Psychotherapy Treatment Planner,** Second Edition
0-471-34764-7 / $44.95

❏ **The Adolescent Psychotherapy Treatment Planner,** Second Edition
0-471-34766-3 / $44.95

❏ **The Addiction Treatment Planner,** Second Edition
0-471-41814-5 / $44.95

❏ **The Couples Psychotherapy Treatment Planner**
0-471-24711-1 / $44.95

❏ **The Group Therapy Treatment Planner**
0-471-37449-0 / $44.95

❏ **The Family Therapy Treatment Planner**
0-471-34768-X / $44.95

❏ **The Older Adult Psychotherapy Treatment Planner**
0-471-29574-4 / $44.95

❏ **The Employee Assistance (EAP) Treatment Planner**
0-471-24709-X / $44.95

❏ **The Gay and Lesbian Psychotherapy Treatment Planner**
0-471-35080-X / $44.95

❏ **The Crisis Counseling and Traumatic Events Treatment Planner**
0-471-39587-0 / $44.95

❏ **The Social Work and Human Services Treatment Planner**
0-471-37741-4 / $44.95

❏ **The Continuum of Care Treatment Planner**
0-471-19568-5 / $44.95

❏ **The Behavioral Medicine Treatment Planner**
0-471-31923-6 / $44.95

❏ **The Mental Retardation and Developmental Disability Treatment Planner**
0-471-38253-1 / $44.95

❏ **The Special Education Treatment Planner**
0-471-38872-6 / $44.95

❏ **The Severe and Persistent Mental Illness Treatment Planner**
0-471-35945-9 / $44.95

❏ **The Personality Disorders Treatment Planner**
0-471-39403-3 / $44.95

❏ **The Rehabilitation Psychology Treatment Planner**
0-471-35178-4 / $44.95

❏ **The Pastoral Counseling Treatment Planner**
0-471-25416-9 / $44.95

❏ **The Juvenile Justice Treatment Planner**
0-471-43320-9 / $44.95

❏ **The Psychiatric Evaluation & Psychopharmacology Treatment Planner**
0-471-43322-5 / $44.95 (available 2/02)

❏ **The Adult Corrections Treatment Planner**
0-471-20244-4 / $44.95 (available 6/02)

❏ **The School Counseling and School Social Work Treatment Planner**
0-471-08496-4 / $44.95 (available 8/02)

Progress Notes Planners contain complete prewritten progress notes for each presenting problem in the companion Treatment Planners.

❏ **The Adult Psychotherapy Progress Notes Planner**
0-471-34763-9 / $44.95

❏ **The Adolescent Psychotherapy Progress Notes Planner**
0-471-38104-7 / $44.95

❏ **The Child Psychotherapy Progress Notes Planner**
0-471-38102-0 / $44.95

❏ **The Addiction Progress Notes Planner**
0-471-09158-8/ $44.95

Name_____

Affiliation_____

Address_____

City/State/Zip_____

Phone/Fax_____

E-mail_____

On the web: practiceplanners.wiley.com

To order, call 1-800-225-5945
(Please refer to promo #1-4019 when ordering.)

Or send this page with payment* to:
John Wiley & Sons, Inc., Attn: J. Knott
605 Third Avenue, New York, NY 10158-0012

❏ Check enclosed ❏ Visa ❏ MasterCard ❏ American Express

Card #_____

Expiration Date_____

Signature_____

*Please add your local sales tax to all orders.

Grief Counseling Homework Planner

PRACTICE *PLANNERS*® SERIES

Treatment *Planners*

The Chemical Dependence Treatment Planner
The Continuum of Care Treatment Planner
The Couples Psychotherapy Treatment Planner
The Employee Assistance Treatment Planner
The Pastoral Counseling Treatment Planner
The Older Adult Psychotherapy Treatment Planner
The Complete Adult Psychotherapy Treatment Planner, 2e
The Behavioral Medicine Treatment Planner
The Group Therapy Treatment Planner
The Gay and Lesbian Psychotherapy Treatment Planner
The Child Psychotherapy Treatment Planner, 2e
The Adolescent Psychotherapy Treatment Planner, 2e
The Family Therapy Treatment Planner
The Severe and Persistent Mental Illness Treatment Planner
The Mental Retardation and Developmental Disability Treatment Planner
The Social Work and Human Services Treatment Planner
The Crisis Counseling and Traumatic Events Treatment Planner
The Personality Disorders Treatment Planner
The Rehabilitation Psychology Treatment Planner
The Addiction Treatment Planner, 2e
The Special Education Treatment Planner

Progress Notes *Planners*

The Child Psychotherapy Progress Notes Planner
The Adolescent Psychotherapy Progress Notes Planner
The Adult Psychotherapy Progress Notes Planner

Homework *Planners*

Brief Therapy Homework Planner
Brief Couples Therapy Homework Planner
Chemical Dependence Treatment Homework Planner
Brief Child Therapy Homework Planner
Brief Adolescent Therapy Homework Planner
Brief Employee Assistance Homework Planner
Brief Family Therapy Homework Planner
Grief Counseling Homework Planner

Documentation *Sourcebooks*

The Clinical Documentation Sourcebook
The Forensic Documentation Sourcebook
The Psychotherapy Documentation Primer
The Chemical Dependence Treatment Documentation Sourcebook
The Clinical Child Documentation Sourcebook
The Couple and Family Clinical Documentation Sourcebook
The Clinical Documentation Sourcebook, 2e
The Continuum of Care Clinical Documentation Sourcebook

PracticePlanners®

Arthur E. Jongsma, Jr., Series Editor

Grief Counseling
Homework Planner

Phil Rich

JOHN WILEY & SONS, INC.

New York • Chichester • Weinheim • Brisbane • Singapore • Toronto

Library of Congress Cataloging-in-Publication Data:

Rich, Phil.
    Grief counseling homework planner / Phil Rich.
        p. cm.—(Practice planners series)
    Includes bibliographical references.
    ISBN 0-471-43318-7 (pbk./disk : alk. paper)
    1. Grief therapy—Handbooks, manuals, etc.   I. Title. II. Practice planners.

RC455.4.L67 R53 2001
616.89'14—dc21   2001023754

Printed in the United States of America.

16 15 14 13

CONTENTS

SERIES PREFACE

The practice of psychotherapy has a dimension that did not exist 30, 20, or even 15 years ago—accountability. Treatment programs, public agencies, clinics, and even group and solo practitioners must now justify the treatment of patients to outside review entities that control the payment of fees. This development has resulted in an explosion of paperwork.

Clinicians must now document what has been done in treatment, what is planned for the future, and what the anticipated outcomes of the interventions are. The books and software in this Practice *Planners* series are designed to help practitioners fulfill these documentation requirements efficiently and professionally.

The Practice *Planners* series is growing rapidly. It now includes not only the second editions of the *Complete Adult Psychotherapy Treatment Planner,* the *Child Psychotherapy Treatment Planner,* and the *Adolescent Psychotherapy Treatment Planner,* but also Treatment Planners targeted to specialty areas of practice, including chemical dependency, the continuum of care, couples therapy, employee assistance, behavioral medicine, therapy with older adults, pastoral counseling, family therapy, group therapy, neuropsychology, therapy with gays and lesbians, and more.

In addition to the Treatment Planners, the series also includes Thera*Scribe*®, the latest version of the popular treatment planning and patient record-keeping software, as well as adjunctive books—such as the *Brief, Chemical Dependence, Couple, Child,* and *Adolescent Therapy Homework Planners;* the *Psychotherapy Documentation Primer;* and the *Clinical, Forensic, Child, Couples and Family, Continuum of Care,* and *Chemical Dependence Documentation Sourcebooks*—containing forms and resources to aid in mental health practice management. The goal of the series is to provide practitioners with the resources they need in order to provide high-quality care in the era of accountability—or, to put it simply, we seek to help you spend more time on patients, and less time on paperwork.

ARTHUR E. JONGSMA, JR.
Grand Rapids, Michigan

INTRODUCTION

Homework provides many benefits for both the therapy client and the therapist. Therapeutic homework extends treatment experiences outside of the session, keeps alive the ideas and feelings expressed during sessions, keeps clients thinking about and focused on therapeutic issues, allows clients to take more responsibility for their own growth and development, and empowers clients to discover their own strengths and limitations. Therapy homework allows for a meaningful extension of treatment that simply cannot take place during the limited time allowed by an individual session. Homework allows clients virtually unlimited time to work on and more fully develop ideas raised in therapy, to contemplate their own thoughts and feelings, and to reflect on and plan for future sessions. Homework thus extends the benefits and power of the therapy far beyond the traditional therapeutic hour.

WHY HOMEWORK?

In an era of time-limited (and often managed) treatment, the Homework Planner adds an additional dimension to therapy and helps make it more cost-effective and focused by the following means:

- Providing a developmental and linear framework for therapeutic grief work

- Directing clients to think about what they want to concentrate on and get out of therapy

- Assigning therapeutic tasks for clients to work on between and before planned sessions

- Preparing clients for individual therapy sessions

- Helping clients develop *contemplative* and *processing* skills

- Allowing clients to develop self-management skills and recognize that they are capable of problem analysis and resolution on their own

- Providing clients with a permanent and important record of the issues they have addressed in treatment and a set of self-reflection skills they can turn to and depend on after their therapy has ended.

ABOUT *GRIEF COUNSELING HOMEWORK PLANNER*

Grief Counseling Homework Planner is designed to help bereaved clients deal with and work through a difficult time in their lives. It provides information about grief and the grieving process and provides a way for bereaved clients to work through the issues surrounding their loss, teaching the skills and techniques of reflective thought, personal management, problem resolution, and self-healing.

FOR WHOM IS *GRIEF COUNSELING HOMEWORK PLANNER* INTENDED?

There are many causes of grief, and many forms. Although *Grief Counseling Homework Planner* is intended primarily for those experiencing grief resulting from the death of someone close, it can nevertheless help clients deal with loss no matter what its source. Many individuals grappling with grief issues of any kind can benefit from a homework approach to grief work and the resolution of grief issues.

Many people experiencing grief will neither seek out nor require therapy. Many others, however, will already be in a therapeutic relationship or will seek out counseling of some form. Although *Grief Counseling Homework Planner* can be used entirely as a self-help book, it is intended to augment individual therapy, not replace it.

USING *GRIEF COUNSELING HOMEWORK PLANNER* IN THERAPY

Homework exercises, regardless of whether they are intended for use in direct conjunction with therapy, prompt exploration and discovery. The process of completing the homework exercises can itself prove an effective means of gaining insight and achieving growth.

When used in conjunction with individual, family, couples, or group therapy, homework exercises both strengthen and are strengthened by the treatment. The process of completing homework exercises can echo and guide the phases of individual therapy. In addition, the use of homework exercises as part of therapy promotes discussion of issues of trust, honesty, and the therapeutic relationship. Clinicians can gauge their clients' willingness to open up or explore areas where the alliance needs strengthening, based on the degree to which the clients are willing to complete and share their homework exercises.

In addition, *Grief Counseling Homework Planner* provides important information that can help clients better understand the grief process and the process of grief work. It also provides a means for clients to identify, address, and work through grief-related problems and issues.

Each section of *Grief Counseling Homework Planner* contains several blank homework exercises to teach, direct, and foster self-expression and self-reflection. However, homework exercises vary in technique as well as content, and different homework exercises are appropriate for different problem sets and stages in grief work. Part of the art and skill of conducting therapy lies in knowing when and how to help clients tackle the issues they are facing. In the case of *Grief Counseling Homework Planner,* this means knowing which exercises to select and when. Accordingly, therapists using *Grief Coun-*

seling Homework Planner must be familiar enough with the homework exercises to know when they are likely to be useful, and when they may be counterproductive. Once therapists are familiar with *Grief Counseling Homework Planner,* they will adapt it to their own theoretical approaches and styles of therapy.

ABOUT THE HOMEWORK EXERCISES

Homework exercises in *Grief Counseling Homework Planner* are never intended to provide answers for clients or to steer them toward the "right" answers. Each of the exercises is intended to teach the skills of self-reflection, exploration, and expression and help clients create their own answers and questions and bring them back to therapy. Clearly, homework exercises push clients into particular directions, but the goal is both self-discovery and the enhancement and extension of in-person therapy sessions.

The type and format of the homework exercises change often. Some exercises are built around checklists, some are very structured, and some provide little structure or are open ended. Most exercises can be completed independently of the others, although within each section it makes most sense to complete the homework exercises in the order presented.

REPEATING EXERCISES

Many of the exercises in *Grief Counseling Homework Planner* are intended or appropriate for multiple use. These exercises can be used by clients repeatedly, either to explore different aspects of their lives, thoughts, and feelings, or to revisit the same treatment issues over and over as they come to understand and process treatment issues more thoroughly. In many instances, clients should be encouraged to complete the same exercise again, or be reassigned the same exercise, whenever it will assist in better understanding an issue, feeling, or thought. In some cases, the exercise should be reassigned if clients have not put adequate effort, energy, time, thought, or honesty into their work.

CAUTION IN USING EXERCISES

Any homework exercise may evoke strong feelings in the client, given the very nature of grief. Nevertheless, some homework exercises are more basic than others and are unlikely to evoke especially difficult emotions in the client. Others, however, drive deeper and may touch emotionally painful areas. In these cases, there is a risk that clients may not be ready for such exercises, or a particular homework exercise may be contraindicated at that point in the treatment process.

THE ORGANIZING MODEL: THREE STAGES OF GRIEF

Grief Counseling Homework Planner is built on a developmental model of the grief process, in which grief work is conceptualized as a three-stage model. The organization of the Homework Planner follows this model, which is briefly reviewed here, and is explained to clients in more detail on the "Setting Perspective" page in Section I.

Stage 1: Acclimation and adjustment.   In this first stage, the tasks largely involve dealing with the initial emotional shock and disorientation often brought by death.

- Adjusting to changes brought by the loss
- Functioning appropriately in daily life
- Keeping emotions and behaviors in check
- Accepting support

Stage 2: Emotional immersion and deconstruction.   In Stage 2, although the initial impact of the death has passed, emotions are often deeply felt. During this stage, bereaved individuals must face and deal with the changes that the death has brought, and often face challenges to their beliefs about the way things should be.

- Contending with reality
- Development of insight
- Reconstructing personal values and beliefs
- Accepting changes and feelings and letting go

Stage 3: Reclamation and reconciliation.   In this final stage many issues about the death have been resolved, and the bereaved more fully begin to reclaim and move on with their lives.

- Development of social relations
- Decisions about changes in lifestyle
- Renewal of self-awareness
- Acceptance of responsibility

Even though *Grief Counseling Homework Planner* was designed to be used in a straight-line sequence following this three-stage model, each section is written as a stand-alone item that can be used independently of other sections, and the same is true of most homework exercises within each section. This allows clients and therapists maximum flexibility to select sections and homework exercises that most fit the immediate situation.

DIRECTIONS FOR THE THERAPIST

Each section opens with a brief description of the type of exercises in the section. Within the section, each homework exercise is preceded by a "Therapist's Overview" subsection, which includes a brief overview of the exercise and its purpose, types of situations for which the exercise may be most useful, and suggestions for processing the exercise with clients. Individual homework exercises immediately follow the therapist's overview.

Preceding the actual homework exercises, the material and homework in each section is briefly explained to the client in a "Setting Perspective" subsection, generally on a single page. This material provides a basic description that will help clients understand the focus of the exercises, and also the ideas and grief work to be developed and worked on through the exercises and this stage of treatment. Therapists should become familiar with the setting perspective material in each section and encourage clients to read the material prior to completing homework exercises.

THERAPISTS' USE OF *GRIEF COUNSELING HOMEWORK PLANNER*

The sections and homework exercises in *Grief Counseling Homework Planner* were designed to be used in sequence, following the three-stage grief model previously described, and exercises within each section are connected and often interrelated. But, if familiar with the book, therapists may choose to create their own sequences of connected exercises. Used this way, therapists may ask clients to work on specific homework exercises that seem to fit a need at that moment in therapy, or assign a connected series of homework exercises.

Alternatively, some therapists may build their entire treatment around *Grief Counseling Homework Planner,* following the three-stage grief model and sequence of the book, by asking clients to use what they learn about themselves through homework exercises as the basis for sessions.

However, although *Grief Counseling Homework Planner* is intended as a direct adjunct to therapy, some therapists may choose simply to recommend *Grief Counseling Homework Planner* to their clients as a source for self-expression and personal growth, independent of what happens in therapy, in effect using it as bibliotherapy.

WORKING AT THE CLIENT'S SKILL LEVEL

Grief Counseling Homework Planner is intended to help clients express themselves and learn *how* to express themselves. The object is to teach self-reflection and self-expression skills, as well as the creativity to write with insight. Nevertheless, some clients will be better able to express themselves in writing than others. However, the goal is not the production of literary masterpieces, but the use and completion of homework that serves as an aid to personal development and as an adjunct to treatment.

CONCLUSION

Your use of *Grief Counseling Homework Planner* will probably be influenced by many factors: the treatment location (inpatient, outpatient, residential care, intensive outpatient treatment, etc.), the client's ability to work on difficult material without regressing, and the stage in therapy, to name but a few variables.

Under any treatment conditions, homework exercises can serve as a valuable adjunct to cost-effective and time-limited treatment, and they are of special value in the managed care environment in which many therapists are already working. The need to extend treatment outside of the boundaries of the therapist's office makes the use of the therapeutic homework still more important.

If the ultimate goal of all therapy is to help clients learn to do without the therapist, then your use of *Grief Counseling Homework Planner* has still more value, as it makes it clear in your work with your clients that the work is *theirs*. By making it clear to clients from the outset that the healing journey is *their* journey, you increase the chances that upon termination your clients will be able to continue on their journeys under their own direction.

Grief Counseling Homework Planner

Section I

STAGES OF GRIEF

There are two exercises in this section. This section describes grief and the grieving process, as well as the nature of grief work. This section provides a three-stage model for understanding the grieving process, and describes each stage in some detail. The primary goals of this section are to provide information to clients and to help clients figure out where they are in the grieving process.

PURPOSE

The information provided gives clients a means for understanding the grief continuum and assessing their own place along this continuum. The three-stage model was briefly described previously, but is explained to clients in more detail in the Setting Perspective subsection.

TYPES OF SITUATIONS FOR WHICH THIS INFORMATION MAY BE MOST USEFUL

- Helping clients to understand the concept and process of grief work
- Helping clients to think about and explore a framework by which to understand the grief process as a whole
- Helping clients to think about their own emotional condition, with respect to the grief process
- Helping clients to understand the work that may lie ahead, as well as any grief work they've already completed
- Helping clients to think about their own place along the grief continuum

STAGES OF GRIEF

The process of working through grief—dealing with the emotions and the situations caused by a death, as well as the impact of the loss on mind, body, and spirit—is frequently referred to as *grief work*.

But although grief experiences are intensely personal, there are some fairly typical stages of bereavement. These range from initial shock, to anguish and despair once the realization of the loss sinks in, to eventual acceptance. Within each stage are specific emotional and psychological tasks which must be worked through completely before you can move on to successfully complete the tasks of the next stage.

Although these stages are generally a predictable part of the mourning process, grief doesn't always move in a straight line. The stages tend to flow together and fluctuate, so it's not always possible to tell which stage you are in. Emotions seesaw, and overwhelming feelings pass and then return. Moods wash in and out like the tide. Just when you think you are over it, a sound, smell, or image can send you back into emotional turmoil. This back-and-forth movement may occur over a period of months, or even years. Although varying from person to person, it's not unusual for the active stages of grieving to last 1 to 2 full years or more.

Becoming aware of the stages of grief can help you to work through the necessary grief work, which includes the following tasks:

- Facing the reality of your loss
- Working through painful memories
- Experiencing the full range of emotions associated with loss
- Coping with the situational and lifestyle changes resulting from your loss
- Adapting to the loss, and reconfiguring your life

THE THREE STAGES OF GRIEF

The goal of grief work is not to find ways to avoid or bypass the emotional turmoil and upsets brought by your loss. Instead, its goals involve working through the tasks and emotions of each stage of grief.

- Stage 1: Acclimation and adjustment
- Stage 2: Emotional immersion and deconstruction
- Stage 3: Reclamation and reconciliation

Stage 1 is a period of *acclimation and adjustment,* in which the primary issues you face as someone newly bereaved can be broken down into four tasks:

- *Adjusting.* Accepting that your loved one is gone, and making sense of the new set of circumstances in your life.

- *Functioning.* It's a cruel irony that the practicalities of mortgage payments, funeral experiences, insurance claims, hospital bills, disbursement of possessions, or getting back to work hit you at a time when you are least up to facing these issues. But despite your loss, you need to accept that you still have a life to lead, and must continue to deal with your everyday responsibilities.

- *Keeping in check.* The temptation in the face of a tremendous loss is to emotionally shut down, or, at the other extreme, to let your emotions and behaviors flow unchecked. One of the tasks of Stage 1 is to find a way to manage your thoughts, feelings, and behaviors.

- *Accepting support.* Often, you don't have to face your loss alone. Learning to accept the kindness, help, encouragement, and support of the friends, family, and others who populate your life is important.

Stage 2 is a time of *Emotional Immersion and Deconstruction,* and incorporates the most active aspects of grief work. It's not that this stage is any more intense than the first stage—in fact, it's difficult to imagine that anything could be more intense than the period immediately following a loss. But during Stage 2, you're likely to become deeply immersed in your feelings and very internally focused. It's also quite common to undergo a *deconstruction* of your values and beliefs, as you question why your loved one was taken from you. The tasks associated with Stage 2 include the following:

- *Contending with reality.* Once the shock of the death has passed, you must begin to more fully resume your normal life, accept that your loved one is gone, and deal with the life changes resulting from your loss.

- *Development of insight.* Stage 2 is a time for soul searching—the exploration of your place in the world, your current emotional state, and the meaning of your thoughts and feelings.

- *Reconstructing personal values and beliefs.* In the aftermath of the death and the many changes it may have brought, you need to find meaning in the world and establish what is—and isn't—important in your life.

- *Acceptance and letting go.*   Here the task is to fully accept the death and your feelings about it, find a way to let go of that which has passed, and begin to move toward that which will be.

Stage 3 is a time for *reclamation and reconciliation,* and is generally thought to be marked by your "recovery" from grief. But the loss of someone close to you leaves a permanent mark on your life, in the sense that things can't be restored to the way they were before the death. However, you can begin to rebuild, creating a new life for yourself and reengaging with the world around you. As this stage ends, you'll become reconciled to the death itself, and the changes it's brought to your life. Perhaps most important, you'll begin to live in the present, rather than the past, reestablish who you are in the world, and plan a future. The primary tasks of this stage are the following:

- *Development of social relations.*   Stage 2 was internally focused, but Stage 3 is externally focused, as you reestablish friendships and renew community connections.
- *Decisions about changes in lifestyle.*   The task here is to make long-term practical choices about how to proceed with your life, including where to live, how to spend your time, what to keep from your old life, and what to change.
- *Renewal of self-awareness.*   This task involves consolidating the things you've learned about yourself and your life through your grief work, and building your daily life around this new self-awareness,
- *Acceptance of responsibility.*   The task here is to both maintain your support network and become increasingly self-reliant, taking responsibility for your own happiness, well-being, and life course.

STAGES OF GRIEF: GETTING LOCATED

GOALS OF THE EXERCISE

This is a simple exercise designed to help clients think about and identity their current grief stage, as well as the grief-work tasks associated with each stage.

TYPES OF SITUATIONS FOR WHICH THIS EXERCISE MAY BE MOST USEFUL

This exercise will help clients think about their current grief-work stage, thus helping them identity the sort of emotional, behavioral, and life-management tasks they may have already completed, are facing at the moment, or are yet to face. This is an especially useful exercise for helping therapists and clients identify current concerns and issues, and for setting the pace for ongoing therapy.

SUGGESTIONS FOR PROCESSING THIS EXERCISE WITH CLIENTS

- Does the idea that there are stages to grief fit your own experience with bereavement?
- Are you able to identity and recognize your current grief work stage?
- What are the grief-work tasks you most need to work on right now?
- Are you feeling encouraged, or does the grief work ahead seem overwhelming?
- Are you aware of the difference between thoughts and feelings?
- Which tasks seem most pressing right now?
- Which tasks seem the most overwhelming or difficult to think about?

STAGES OF GRIEF: GETTING LOCATED

Based on the descriptions of the grief continuum and the stages of grief, circle the letter that most closely describes where you are *right now* with each task: A = I'm not ready to deal with this task; B = I'm working on this task; C = I've completed this task.

Stage 1 Tasks

Adjusting	A	B	C
Functioning	A	B	C
Keeping in check	A	B	C
Accepting support	A	B	C

Stage 2 Tasks

Contending with reality	A	B	C
Development of insight	A	B	C
Reconstructing personal values and beliefs	A	B	C
Acceptance and letting go	A	B	C

Stage 3 Tasks

Development of social relations	A	B	C
Decisions about changes in life style	A	B	C
Renewal of self-awareness	A	B	C
Acceptance of responsibility	A	B	C

You're now aware of the stages of grief and how they typically progress, with respect to each of the emotional and practical tasks of grief work. Look at the answers you've circled above:

1. Which four tasks are the most relevant to you *now*, in your current grief stage?

_____

_____

_____

_____

2. What do the tasks you've picked tell you about your current grief work?

_____

_____

_____

_____

3. What's your current grief stage? (If it's difficult for you to easily identify your current grief stage, go directly to the next question.)

_____

4. Was it difficult for you to easily identify your current grief stage? If so, why?

_____

_____

_____

_____

5. What are your *thoughts* as you complete this exercise?
   I'm thinking

_____

_____

_____

_____

6. What are your *feelings* as you complete this exercise?
   I'm feeling

_____

_____

_____

_____

Remember to bring the completed worksheet to your next appointment.

IDENTIFYING YOUR FEELINGS

GOALS OF THE EXERCISE

This is a checklist-based exercise that will help clients identity immediate and significant feelings and concerns, providing important information to the therapist regarding the most pressing issues to be addressed in therapy

TYPES OF SITUATIONS FOR WHICH THIS EXERCISE MAY BE MOST USEFUL

This exercise will help in understanding the client's current emotional state with respect to grief management and grief work, as well as in differential diagnosis, including diagnosis of significant mental health concerns such as depression, Posttraumatic Stress Disorder (PTSD), anxiety disorders, and the like.

SUGGESTIONS FOR PROCESSING THIS EXERCISE WITH CLIENTS

- Are there specific questions you need to answer for yourself before continuing with your grief work?

- Do you have a clear sense of the sorts of issues, feelings, and tasks that you'll be facing in your grief work?

- Have you ever experienced feelings of this sort before?

- Why do you think you're having these particular feelings?

- Are you afraid your feelings will never pass?

- Are the problems you're experiencing so severe or debilitating that you're having trouble functioning in your day-to-day life?

- How did you feel as you were completing the exercise?

IDENTIFYING YOUR FEELINGS

Check all of the emotional states that best describe how you are generally feeling at this point in your bereavement.

____ Afraid	You're scared of what life will be like now. You may be fearful about your ability to cope emotionally, or you may be uncertain about practical concerns like money, raising the children, or where you'll live. You may just feel afraid, without really knowing why.
____ Angry	Anger often feels like a physical thing. Your muscles tense up, and you may feel like yelling at someone or hitting something. Your rage may be aimed at yourself or your lost loved one, or you may find yourself getting angry at other people, society, or your spiritual beliefs.
____ Anxious	Anxiety is distinct from fear, and is often a generalized feeling. If you're afraid, at least you know what scares you. If you're anxious, on the other hand, you're likely to feel agitated without knowing exactly why. You may experience cold sweats, hyperactivity, or edginess.
____ Ashamed	You may feel that you should be getting over your feelings, or may be ashamed to show them in front of family, friends, and others. You may also harbor feelings about the death, or the fact that you are still alive, that feel shameful to you and are difficult to share with others.
____ Bitter	Life may feel very unjust, and you may feel cheated and disappointed. You may feel jealous and resentful toward others who still have what has been taken from you, and you may feel victimized by fate.
____ Confused	You may be unsure of what you're feeling, or your feelings may change quickly. Your thoughts may be unfocused, and it may be difficult to concentrate; or you may have a hard time knowing what to do and how best to make decisions.

_____ Depressed

Depression can be a general mood of melancholy, or a full-blown experience that is all-encompassing and seems to have no end. In a major depression your mood, appetite, sleep, memory, and ability to concentrate are seriously impaired. You may feel the impulse to do self-destructive things in an effort to find relief.

_____ Despairing

Here you feel a sense of futility. It seems as though things will never get better, and the distress caused by the death may feel unbearable. Although you want to, you may not be able to get your feelings out by crying, or you may be unable to stop crying.

_____ Detached

You feel disconnected from the death and detached from life in general. The experience seems unreal, as if it were happening to someone else. You simply pass through life each day, your actions detached from your thoughts and feelings.

_____ Guilty

You may feel that you could have done more to help your loved one or to prevent the death. You may feel intense regret about the way you behaved toward your loved one, or promises you never kept. You may also feel guilty about negative feelings you harbor toward your loved one, or mixed feelings about the death itself. It is also common for the bereaved to feel guilty when they begin to laugh and find pleasure in life once again, or begin new relationships. Or you may experience survival guilt—a sense of remorse that you remain alive while your loved one has died.

_____ Helpless

Things seem out of your control. You may think that if you were powerless to prevent the death, then you can't handle anything. You can't cope with the practicalities of everyday life, and feel unable to control or manage your feelings.

_____ Hopeless

Life has no meaning. It seems there is no point to anything, and things will never get better. Your feelings and the tasks you face seem insurmountable, and you feel unable to ever overcome your loss.

_____ Lonely

There is no one that can understand your pain. There seems to be no one to share things with or seek comfort from. These feelings may make you feel like withdrawing even further from those around you, or from the world at large.

_____ Lost

Everything that you used to believe in is gone. You aren't sure where you fit in the world, or who you are. If you are religious or spiritual, your faith is shaken. If you are not, you feel it unwise to ever have faith in a world where nothing seems permanent.

_____ Numb · You are shut down emotionally. You feel nothing. Everything is flat. Although you might be able to function and get through each day, it sometimes seems as if you are sleepwalking through life, unable to feel your emotions.

_____ Sad · Sorrow and heartbreak color everything. You feel your loss deeply, and it affects and pervades all you do. It is a mood that simply won't go away.

_____ Shocked · You are bewildered and confused. Even if you were prepared for the death, the situation doesn't seem real. The finality of the situation leaves you feeling stunned, and you may not be able to accept that your loved one is gone. You keep hoping to wake up from a bad dream.

_____ Overwhelmed · You simply can't cope with the barrage of emotions, thoughts, and changes facing you. You feel like running away, or escaping by using alcohol or drugs. You want someone to come and rescue you, and make it all go away.

_____ Preoccupied · You can't stop thinking about your loss. Perhaps you keep replaying certain scenes over and over in your mind, or agonize about who you might lose next. You can't concentrate on your everyday responsibilities or engage in a conversation without your mind wandering. Intrusive memories keep surfacing no matter what you do.

_____ Vulnerable · Your faith in your own invulnerability is shattered. You are constantly aware of your own mortality, and the mortality of other important people in your life. You feel exposed, without protection, to whatever destiny or life hands you.

_____ Yearning · You long for the deceased. It hurts so much that you feel a constant pit in your stomach. You are constantly aware of the absence of your loved one, and you feel empty. Nothing can fill the void.

Of the feelings you checked off, which three are most intense right now?

1. _____

2. _____

3. _____

Complete these five sentences:

1. As I complete this section, I feel like . . .

   _____

   _____

   _____

2. Right now, I'd like to . . .

   _____

   _____

   _____

3. Lately, I've been feeling like . . .

   _____

   _____

   _____

4. My most important current task is . . .

   _____

   _____

   _____

5. I feel like I most need to work on . . .

   _____

   _____

   _____

Remember to bring the completed worksheet to your next appointment.

Section II

ACCOMMODATION AND ADJUSTMENT

There are four exercises in this section. This section deals with Stage 1 issues in grief work. The exercises in this section focus on acclimation, adjustment, and self-expression. They can help clients to examine and begin to talk about their loss, and thus begin to accept and adjust to the feelings and changes brought by the death of a loved one.

PURPOSE

The information and exercises will help clients recognize the importance of bringing the death into the open, outside of themselves, where they can begin to confront and explore its reality.

TYPES OF SITUATIONS FOR WHICH THIS INFORMATION MAY BE MOST USEFUL

The information will be useful in helping to orient clients who have only recently experienced a significant loss, and in giving clients a sense of perspective and an overview of the grief work at this early stage.

The information is equally important for clients who have been unable to deal with, adjust to, or make accommodations for a loss and are continuing to struggle with the earliest stages of adjustment although the death occurred weeks or months ago.

ACCOMMODATION AND ADJUSTMENT

The first goal in your grief work is to *accommodate* your loss—to find a way to accept it, and begin adjusting to the changes it's brought to your life. This is an important early step; but like most facets of grief work, it's sometimes easier said than done. Ultimately, there's no way to fake adjustment, and no way around the pain that accompanies it. Your grief work at this stage largely centers around allowing the full impact of the death to sink in. A second important aspect of adjustment is finding a means of expressing your thoughts and feelings in a way that prevents you from becoming stuck in your current emotions.

You must find a way to think and talk about your loss—to get these things outside of your head. The capacity to express thoughts and feelings is a crucial component of recovery from any trauma. But you may not be ready to talk to others about the depth of your feelings. Or you may feel you have no one to tell, or that others won't want to hear everything you have to say. It may also be true that you don't know what to say, or how to say it.

Much of *Grief Counseling Homework Planner* is about developing your skills in self-reflection and expression. The homework exercises allow you to have a conversation with yourself—even if you aren't comfortable with sharing your thoughts or deepest feelings with others. You may well find that writing about these difficult emotional experiences will be cathartic—that you can unburden yourself by putting words to your feelings and giving a voice to your thoughts.

The first step in managing difficult feelings and overcoming obstacles is to face them. In these earliest days of your adjustment, thinking and writing about your loss, even if you're not fully ready to talk about it, will help you to confront it and begin to take the reality of the death into your life. Describing your feelings and the circumstances of the death will help you develop internal strength, and will provide a framework on which your later grief work can build.

THESE EARLY DAYS

GOALS OF THE EXERCISE

Using sentence starts, this exercise helps the client to think and write about early and current reactions to the loss.

TYPES OF SITUATIONS FOR WHICH THIS EXERCISE MAY BE MOST USEFUL

This exercise will help the client think about and begin to process thoughts and feelings related to the loss. In addition, the exercise will help the therapist identify thoughts or feelings that may flag significant underlying diagnoses, such as depression, anxiety, or PTSD.

SUGGESTIONS FOR PROCESSING THIS EXERCISE WITH CLIENTS

- Was it difficult to write about some of your loss experiences?
- Did the writing come easier than you thought it might, or was it hard to find words?
- Was writing a positive, negative, or neutral experience?
- Did the writing prompt other thoughts, feelings, or reactions? If it did, what will you do with them?
- What were your first reactions to the death?
- What was the most pressing thought or feeling raised by the exercise?
- What has been the most difficult thing to adjust to since the death?
- Why is this thing the most difficult to deal with?

THESE EARLY DAYS

Sentence "starts" are a good way to help you write when you feel a little stuck. They provide a kick start to help you focus on your feelings and thoughts.

Complete these sentence starts, after first taking a few moments to think about the words that best describe your reactions, feelings, or thoughts.

1. When I learned of the death I felt . . .

   _____

   _____

   _____

   _____

2. My reaction to the death was to . . .

   _____

   _____

   _____

   _____

3. After the death I . . .

   _____

   _____

   _____

   _____

4. Since the death, I haven't been able to . . .

   _____

   _____

   _____

   _____

5. Since the death, I mostly feel . . .

_____

_____

_____

_____

Beginning with these sentence starts, describe your current feelings in more detail.

1. When I think of the death, I . . .

_____

_____

_____

_____

2. Since the death, my life has changed the most in that . . .

_____

_____

_____

_____

3. Since my loss, I find my life to be . . .

_____

_____

_____

_____

4. Since the death, I most need . . .

_____

_____

_____

_____

Remember to bring the completed worksheet to your next appointment.

EXPRESSING YOURSELF

GOALS OF THE EXERCISE

The exercise allows the client the opportunity to reflect on feelings and thoughts of that moment. The exercise helps the client distinguish between *thoughts* and *feelings*.

TYPES OF SITUATIONS FOR WHICH THIS EXERCISE MAY BE MOST USEFUL

The exercise will help clients free up their feelings and begin to explore ideas, thoughts, and feelings that have been frozen by the loss of a loved one. It will also help clients find words for their feelings and get things out into the open where they can be looked at and discussed.

SUGGESTIONS FOR PROCESSING THIS EXERCISE WITH CLIENTS

* Was there a theme to the sentence starts you chose? What prompted these particular sentence starts? Do they tell you something about the issues most on your mind right now?

* Does it help to get ideas out into the open?

* Do you understand the causes of your feelings, and why you feel that way?

* Do you see a difference between a *thought* and a *feeling?* Can you easily distinguish between your thoughts and your feelings?

* Is there a connection between thoughts and feelings—does one affect the other?

* How important is it to get ideas, thoughts, and feelings out into the open?

* What is most disturbing about getting things out into the open?

* What are you most afraid might happen if you express yourself fully?

EXPRESSING YOURSELF

The previous exercise used sentence starts to help free up your thoughts, feelings, and expression through writing. Sentence starts can also be used as an outline tool—a way to identify the things that you want to explore further.

In this exercise you'll create five sentence starts of your own, using the sentence starts from the previous exercise as examples. Focus each sentence start on some aspect of your feelings or thoughts since your loss. First, create the sentence start but do *not* complete it. Instead, create all five starts and then return and finish each sentence start.

1. Your sentence start: _____

    Now finish the sentence . . . _____

    _____

    _____

    _____

2. Your sentence start: _____

    Now finish the sentence . . . _____

    _____

    _____

    _____

3. Your sentence start: _____

    Now finish the sentence . . . _____

    _____

    _____

    _____

4. Your sentence start: _____

   Now finish the sentence . . . _____

   _____

   _____

   _____

5. Your sentence start: _____

   Now finish the sentence . . . _____

   _____

   _____

   _____

6. How is what you're thinking and writing about affecting the way you feel?
   Right now, I feel . . .

   _____

   _____

   _____

7. Describe the ideas, opinions, and impressions that are going through your head.
   Right now, I'm thinking about . . .

   _____

   _____

   _____

8. *The thing that most keeps me from expressing myself is . . .*

   _____

   _____

   _____

9. *What helps me give voice to my feelings is . . .*

   _____

   _____

   _____

Remember to bring the completed worksheet to your next appointment.

THIS LOSS IN MY LIFE

GOALS OF THE EXERCISE

Many of the exercises in *Grief Counseling Homework Planner* are intended for multiple use—for clients to use repeatedly, either to explore different aspects of their lives, thoughts, and feelings, or to revisit the same treatment issues over and over as they come to understand and process them more thoroughly. This exercise is one of those that is to be repeated more than once. It will help clients consider important aspects of the loss of a loved one, with each exercise focusing on only one aspect of the loss. The primary goals are both self-realization and early adjustment.

TYPES OF SITUATIONS FOR WHICH THIS EXERCISE MAY BE MOST USEFUL

This is a writing exercise for clients to repeat over and over. Like many of the exercises in *Grief Counseling Homework Planner,* the exercise will help clients to get and stay in touch with their thoughts and feelings, and learn to spot and express them.

SUGGESTIONS FOR PROCESSING THIS EXERCISE WITH CLIENTS

- Do you wonder if this part of your loss will ever change? Do you think it will?

- What is the most difficult part of this aspect of your loss to bear?

- How do you feel as you work through this exercise? Is writing about your loss difficult?

- Do you usually ever stop long enough in your daily routine to actually think about your life, and what's weighing on your mind at that moment? What was it like to reflect on your life in this way?

- Will it help to use this exercise again, to think about and express other aspects of your loss, or any other feelings?

THIS LOSS IN MY LIFE

In this exercise, rather than think about your loss in broad terms (its effect on your entire life), you'll focus on only one aspect of it. The exercise will help you explore just *one* part of your feelings—for this reason, you should repeat the exercise more than once, in order to think and write about different aspects of your loss.

1. What three things about your loss are on your mind right now?

   _____

   _____

   _____

2. Which of these three things do you want to explore in writing right now?

   _____

3. Why do you want to write about this part of your loss?

   _____

   _____

   _____

   _____

4. What is the most difficult part of this aspect of your loss?

   _____

   _____

   _____

   _____

5. How does this aspect of your loss make you feel?

_____

_____

_____

_____

6. What is the first thing that comes to mind when you think about this aspect of your loss?

_____

_____

_____

_____

7. What might help you better deal with this part of your loss?

_____

_____

_____

_____

8. What can you do to better adjust to or accept this part of your loss?

_____

_____

_____

_____

One of the advantages of writing down your thoughts is that it gives you a chance to review and reflect on what you've written. Take a moment now to reread what you've just written, and then think about it. Then write down any new thoughts that you may have about your loss, or what you've written.

9. _Right now, I feel . . ._

_____

_____

_____

_____

Remember to bring the completed worksheet to your next appointment.

BARRIERS TO ADJUSTMENT

GOALS OF THE EXERCISE

This brief exercise directs the client to consider what changes are the most difficult changes to adjust to and why. It asks the client to identify obstacles to adjustment.

TYPES OF SITUATIONS FOR WHICH THIS EXERCISE MAY BE MOST USEFUL

Again, this is an exercise to help clients deal with the initial issues of loss and bereavement. It's especially helpful for clients who do not seem to recognize what they most need, who turn away the kind of help and support that might assist them in making a smoother adjustment to this new phase of their lives, or who are unable to recognize what they most need to do themselves in order to make the early adjustment.

SUGGESTIONS FOR PROCESSING THIS EXERCISE WITH CLIENTS

- Are you able to recognize and identify those things that you have special difficulty adjusting to?

- Why are these things so especially difficult to adjust to?

- What are the circumstances or personal factors that most affect your ability to adjust?

- Are there things you should consider as ways to overcome obstacles to adjustment?

- Do you need special help to overcome special problems or obstacles to adjustment? If so, what kind of help—family, friends, clergy, support group?

BARRIERS TO ADJUSTMENT

1. The biggest change I've faced in my life since the death is . . .

   _____

   _____

   _____

   _____

2. The thing I'm having the most trouble adjusting to is . . .

   _____

   _____

   _____

   _____

3. Three things that are interfering with my ability to adjust are . . .

   _____

   _____

   _____

4. Eight things I can do to help me get over these hurdles are . . .

   _____

   _____

   _____

   _____

   _____

   _____

   _____

   _____

Remember to bring the completed worksheet to your next appointment.

Section III

ACCEPTANCE

This section contains four exercises on distinguishing between adjustment and acceptance. The primary focus of this section is on bringing the death of a loved one into daily life and helping clients learn how to both live with the loss and live around it as life continues. There is an increased focus on self-expression and the importance of finding words to express feelings.

PURPOSE

The client information provides clients with an overview of the emotional tasks associated with this early stage in their grief work.

TYPES OF SITUATIONS FOR WHICH THIS SECTION MAY BE MOST USEFUL

This is most helpful for clients who are in the earliest part of the grief work, and it builds on the work of adjustment addressed in the previous section. It will help clients distinguish between acceptance and adjustment, and will help them lay the basis for future grief work that is built on an acceptance of the death. In many ways, dealing with and building acceptance addresses the first four stages of death and dying as described by Elisabeth Kubler-Ross: denial and isolation, anger, bargaining, and depression. Although the three-stage model used here is different in construct, this work addresses the idea that successful and effective grief work is built on the idea of acceptance (the fifth stage in the Kubler-Ross model).

ACCEPTANCE

Acceptance is not the same thing as adjustment. Adjustment is a response and accommodation to change—but *adjusting* to something doesn't actually mean you've *accepted* it.

Acceptance, though, is a word with more than one meaning. Acceptance, for instance, can sometimes mean giving up. That's *not* the kind of acceptance we mean! In this case, acceptance means acknowledging and accepting the reality of a new situation, without fighting that new reality. In the case of your loss, you must accept it. You must give in to the reality of the death of a loved one, because all of your feelings, your regrets, and your behaviors cannot change it. In your grief work, you can change only yourself.

ACCEPTING THE CHANGE

Acceptance will mean different things at different points in your bereavement. In the earliest stages of your grief, acceptance requires only that you acknowledge the reality of the death and accept the changes in your life. Later, acceptance will mean submitting to your feelings and accepting their power. As you work through the final stage of your grief, acceptance will mean concession—your willingness to fully accept the loss and move on.

In many ways, acceptance underpins adjustment. In order to more fully adjust, you have to really work on accepting the death and the changes it has brought.

What sort of things help people accept death? The memorials and customs that follow the immediate loss play several important roles. Funerals, spiritual services, and commemorative gatherings make death very concrete—which is clearly one part of acceptance. They also provide an opportunity for people to vent their feelings, and in most cases almost any display of emotions is okay, and often expected. Eulogies and other spoken memorials allow the bereaved to formally say their goodbyes, and unspoken tributes like flowers allow a symbolic goodbye. The family gatherings that often take place after the funeral allow the mourners to give and receive condolences, talk and exchange memories, and again feel and vent emotions among the people closest to them.

Each of these customs contains the wisdom of folklore. Dealing with death means first accepting its finality; everything that follows is about expressing your grief. These sorts of customs each contain the very things that will help you to accept your loss:

- They make the death very real.

- They remind you that although the body of your loved one has passed, spirit and memory lives on in your life.

- They allow a way to formally say goodbye.
- They provide a public recognition of your loss.
- They provide the opportunity to openly display and vent emotions.
- They allow the load of death to be shared with other mourners.
- They allow you to get emotional support from others.
- They allow you to give emotional support to others.
- They give you the chance to talk about your loss, to reminisce, and to generally talk with others about your loved one.
- They give your support group a chance to see how you're doing over the first days, and to gauge whether more support or help is needed.

RITE OF PASSAGE

GOALS OF THE EXERCISE

This exercise asks for a description of the funeral ceremony, as well as the ways in which the client was affected and moved by it. The exercise ends with any last words which should have been said at the funeral, but weren't.

TYPES OF SITUATIONS FOR WHICH THIS EXERCISE MAY BE MOST USEFUL

This exercise can be used immediately after the funeral ceremony, or weeks after. It is designed both to bring the reality of the death to the surface and to allow a way to focus on the often deeply moving and ritualistic aspects of burial services that can allow a level of both comfort and inspiration, as well as sadness. It provides a way for clients to relive the most moving parts of the ceremony.

SUGGESTIONS FOR PROCESSING THIS EXERCISE WITH CLIENTS

- You've just written about aspects of the funeral that moved you. Were there also aspects that you found disturbing? If there were, will it help to write about them or discuss them?
- Were you able to use the funeral as a place to say goodbye? Did it meet your early needs for comfort and support?
- If there was no funeral, or it seemed inadequate, did you feel able to say goodbye? Is it still important for you to hold a funeral service?
- How important is it to say goodbye? Do you feel that you have been able to say goodbye?
- What is most difficult about saying goodbye?

RITE OF PASSAGE

1. What was the funeral like for you?

_____

_____

_____

_____

2. What words were spoken that affected or inspired you?

_____

_____

_____

_____

3. What other aspects of the funeral affected you?

_____

_____

_____

_____

4. What was the most moving and memorable part of the ceremony?

_____

_____

_____

_____

5. Take a few moments to think back and recall the funeral. Think about it deeply. Think about what the weather was like that day, and the way you felt. Try to recall the mood of the ceremony, and briefly describe it.

_____

_____

_____

_____

6. Describe the ceremony again, focusing on its most moving aspects.

_____

_____

_____

_____

7. Are there any words that should have been said at the funeral, but were not? If there are, say them now.

_____

_____

_____

_____

Remember to bring the completed worksheet to your next appointment.

I STILL CAN'T BELIEVE IT

GOALS OF THE EXERCISE

The clear theme in this exercise is the often head-shaking realization of loss that follows the death of someone close. In this exercise, clients focus on the changes in their world since the death and on how they have been affected emotionally.

TYPES OF SITUATIONS FOR WHICH THIS EXERCISE MAY BE MOST USEFUL

This exercise is helpful for clients who are unable to see or have special difficulty accepting the reality and finality of death. It is also a general useful exercise for all clients as it will help put reality, finality, and feelings into words. It can be used with clients who have experienced recent loss and are still shocked, and with clients who are beginning to recover from the initial shock and impact of the death, but continue to experience that "I still can't believe it" feeling.

SUGGESTIONS FOR PROCESSING THIS EXERCISE WITH CLIENTS

- What is it like to constantly experience your loss, and its reality, each time you realize that things have changed?

- Is it getting easier to accept the loss? Is it remaining difficult? Either way, why?

- Does writing or talking help? If it does, in what ways? Are there other ways you can express yourself and your sorrow?

- Do you have lots of thoughts and feelings about the death that you've never expressed? If so, how are you going to discharge these feelings? Do you want to express them?

I STILL CAN'T BELIEVE IT

There may be times where you find yourself shaking your head and saying "I still can't believe it." There is nothing wrong with that thought—it's completely normal and may go on for a while. At some point, you'll notice a change from "I can't believe this is happening" to "I can't believe this has happened." This will mark the point where you've begun to fully accept the reality of your loss, showing you are moving through your bereavement.

1. How has your world changed since the death?

_____

_____

_____

_____

2. What do you especially miss?

_____

_____

_____

_____

3. What's the hardest thing to accept?

_____

_____

_____

_____

4. What's it like when you realize this really has happened?

_____

_____

_____

_____

5. What makes you the saddest?

_____

_____

_____

_____

6. What makes you the maddest?

_____

_____

_____

_____

Remember to bring the completed worksheet to your next appointment.

REMEMBERING THE DAY

GOALS OF THE EXERCISE

This exercise provides a portrait of the day of the death of the loved one. It asks the client to describe other events of that day, and the events leading to the death.

TYPES OF SITUATIONS FOR WHICH THIS EXERCISE MAY BE MOST USEFUL

This exercise, like others in this section, takes clients back to the death and brings it to the forefront of their thinking and feelings. It is a way to relive and possibly reexperience a difficult experience in order to bring it to the surface, process it, and accept it.

However, for some, the very act of recounting a traumatic event triggers strong emotional reactions, and you should proceed with caution if the story of this death is especially traumatic for your client. If the exercise produces deep feelings that seem unbearable to the client, he or she is not yet ready to write about the death.

SUGGESTIONS FOR PROCESSING THIS EXERCISE WITH CLIENTS

- Was it useful to think and write about the death, and revisit it through the telling of the story? Are there other stories of the death you want to tell?

- Is it important to chronicle these stories? Will it be better for you to write these stories down and keep them so you can return to them at a later time, or are these stories you want to pass on or leave untold?

- Does writing and taking about the death make it more bearable, or somehow help you to integrate it into your everyday life?

REMEMBERING THE DAY

For some, the very act of recounting a traumatic event can trigger all sorts of emotional reactions, and you should proceed with caution if the story of this death is especially traumatic for you. You'll know this as you start to work on your exercise, or even as you think about it. If it produces unbearable feelings, you're not yet ready to write about the death. Come back to the exercise at a later time, or make sure you have someone to talk to as you work on it, in case your writing especially troubles you.

1. What was the day and date of the death?

   _____

   _____

   _____

2. What can you remember about the rest of that day? What was the weather like; was there a significant event in the news; how was the rest of life before you heard the news? What were the details of that day?

   _____

   _____

   _____

   _____

3. Where were you when you learned of the death? What were you doing?

   _____

   _____

   _____

   _____

4. What led up to this loss? Write the story of the death.

_____

_____

_____

_____

5. Did you get a chance to say goodbye?

_____

_____

_____

_____

6. If you could have spoken to your loved one that day, what would you have said? If you did speak that day, what would you now add?

_____

_____

_____

_____

Remember to bring the completed worksheet to your next appointment.

I CHOOSE TO OVERCOME GRIEF

GOALS OF THE EXERCISE

The last exercise in this section aims to further help the client deal with adjustment and acceptance issues. It provides a means for both self-expression and a simple commitment to emotional and physical health through this difficult time.

TYPES OF SITUATIONS FOR WHICH THIS EXERCISE MAY BE MOST USEFUL

This is the last exercise in this section, and is aimed largely at clients who are having difficulty adjusting to and accepting the loss of a loved one. The exercise focuses on the importance of both experiencing and integrating grief in order to build a base for ongoing grief work.

The exercise concludes with a list of "Wills" and "Won'ts," which represent the client's commitment to stay emotionally and physically healthy.

SUGGESTIONS FOR PROCESSING THIS EXERCISE WITH CLIENTS

- What was it like to explore and describe your grief in words?

- Can you both accept and be soothed by grief, and yet also choose to overcome grief?

- What does it mean to you to *overcome* grief?

- Are you able to accept your loss? What has been the most helpful thing in helping you to find acceptance? What has been the most difficult part of acceptance?

- Is it difficult to agree to the Wills and Won'ts? Are you really ready to follow their suggestions as you work your way through grief?

I CHOOSE TO OVERCOME GRIEF

Acceptance begins here:

> *Grant me the serenity to accept the things I cannot change, courage to change the things I can, and wisdom to know the difference.*
> —REINHOLD NIEBUHR

1. Complete these sentence starts: "My grief feels like . . .

   the seasons coming and going *because* . . .

   _____

   _____

   _____

   _____

   a complicated puzzle *because* . . .

   _____

   _____

   _____

   physical pain *because* . . .

   _____

   _____

   _____

   a broken vase *because* . . .

   _____

   _____

   _____

a raging river *because* . . .

_____

_____

_____

2. Complete these sentences:

I embrace my grief by . . .

_____

_____

_____

_____

My grief soothes me by . . .

_____

_____

_____

_____

My grief reminds me that . . .

_____

_____

_____

_____

I choose to overcome my grief because . . .

_____

_____

_____

_____

3. These Wills and Won't's represent your commitment to stay emotionally and physically healthy. *Think about each one before you check off your agreement.*

_____ I will stay active in my daily life.

_____ I will be patient with myself.

_____ I will connect with others.

_____ I will express my feelings.

_____ I will take care of my physical health.

_____ I will seek support if I need it.

_____ I won't expect people to know how I'm feeling if I don't tell them.

_____ I won't try to hide my feelings.

_____ I won't try to predict how long it will take to feel better.

_____ I won't isolate myself.

_____ I won't make any major decisions.

_____ I won't try to escape from my feelings.

Remember to bring the completed worksheet to your next appointment.

Section IV

SUPPORT

This section, consisting of four exercises, describes different types of support, as well as different types and levels of support systems. One goal is to help clients consider their needs for support, and another is to help clients learn how to get the kind of support they need. This is one of several sections that sensitizes clients to their community.

PURPOSE

The client information provides clients with an overview of the emotional tasks associated with this early stage in their grief work.

TYPES OF SITUATIONS FOR WHICH THIS SECTION MAY BE MOST USEFUL

Different kinds of support are both necessary and available to clients, for different reasons and at different times both in their grief work and in their lives in general. Clients who are having difficulty seeking or accepting help, or are not getting or recognizing the full array of support available and necessary, will find these exercises helpful.

SUPPORT

There are many levels of support, from the concerned attitude of work colleagues to the close level of support, and often shared grief, of family members and close friends. Because support comes from different sources and is offered for different reasons, it varies widely in intensity, ability to provide comfort, and level of care provided.

You'll need much support in your bereavement, of different types at different times, and from different people. Through the exercises in this section you'll have the chance to think and write about the kind of support that's available in your life, and where it comes from. Perhaps most important, these homework exercises will help you to understand the kind of help you want and need, and how to get it.

SOURCES OF SUPPORT

You have two kinds of support systems. The first is a *natural* support system group made up of family, friends, and others in your daily life. Your natural support group consists of your *inner circle* of close relatives, friends, and others, and an *outer circle* of neighbors, coworkers, and distant friends. Natural support stems from your family and others in your daily life, and is an automatic response to your loss—people will naturally provide support without your having to seek it out.

You also have available to you a *drafted* support system, which must be developed. Drafted support includes all help that has to be sought out—usually because the natural support system can't meet your needs—from emotional to financial. People in your natural support system are, by definition, in your life, and they can see your loss for themselves— their support flows from this awareness. However, drafted supporters are unaware of your loss until someone seeks them out. It's not that drafted support is any less well-meaning or sincere, but it's a different level and type of support that has to be activated by someone. It's like the difference between first aid delivered on the spot by someone present at the time of an injury, and the care provided by medical practitioners who have to be notified of the injury.

It's important to know that you have both types of support available, and also how to distinguish between the two. It's of equal importance that you understand which type of support you need and how to get it.

THE DAY AFTER

GOALS OF THE EXERCISE

This exercise begins with the first wave of support, and helps to center the client's thinking on what sort of support was most immediately available at the time of the loved one's death, and what sort was, and is, most needed *now*. This exercise will help clients recognize the need for support.

TYPES OF SITUATIONS FOR WHICH THIS EXERCISE MAY BE MOST USEFUL

This exercise will help clients recognize the support that has been available, and will get them ready to think in more detail about the sort of support that is currently needed, and the sort that will be needed in the immediate future.

SUGGESTIONS FOR PROCESSING THIS EXERCISE WITH CLIENTS

- What would the day after the death have been like if you hadn't received support?
- Did you get the kind of support you needed? If you didn't get as much, or the kind of, support needed—why not?
- Are you still getting support, and is it the kind of support you want and need?
- Do you know what kind of support you need?
- Are you satisfied with the sort of support you're getting?
- Do you seek out support? Do you accept support when it is offered?

THE DAY AFTER

Support is probably the most active, and the least organized, in the immediate aftermath of the death of a loved one. Family, friends, neighbors, coworkers, and others in your natural support system are quick to respond, eager to help console you and lighten your burden. Probably the most useful kinds of immediate support include practical help with the daily aspects of your life—looking after the children, walking the dog, and paying the bills—and the emotional support of simply being there.

What was the day after like for you? What kind of support did you get, and how did it feel? Did it ease the pain, and help get you through the day?

1. What sort of support did you most immediately need in the first day, and the day after?

   _____

   _____

   _____

   _____

2. Who was most important in providing support that next day? Who stands out, and why?

   _____

   _____

   _____

   _____

3. Was it important to receive support the next day? If so, why?

   _____

   _____

   _____

   _____

4. What aspect of that support are you most grateful for?

_____

_____

_____

_____

5. What might the next day have been like without support?

_____

_____

_____

_____

Remember to bring the completed worksheet to your next appointment.

THE RIGHT HELP AT THE RIGHT TIME

GOALS OF THE EXERCISE

The theme of the previous exercise is picked up by asking the client to think further about the kind of support available and the kind of support needed. This exercise can help clients address, realize, and get in touch with their particular needs for support and the *sorts* of support they need.

TYPES OF SITUATIONS FOR WHICH THIS EXERCISE MAY BE MOST USEFUL

Exercises like this can help clients recognize not only the general need for support, but their *specific* needs, which will change over time. In some cases, clients may feel that they are complaining about or ungrateful for the support available to them, but the larger focus is to help clients get in touch with and become honest about their needs in order to get those needs met.

SUGGESTIONS FOR PROCESSING THIS EXERCISE WITH CLIENTS

- Is there a difference between what you *want* and what you *need?*
- What kind of support do you most *want?* What kind do you least *want?*
- What kind of support do you most *need?* What kind do you least *need?*
- Are your needs being recognized? If not, what's getting in the way?
- Is your need for support changing as time passes? Do you need a different kind of support now than you did in the days immediately after the death?
- Are you using the support you have, or are you creating your own obstacles to getting support?
- What's it like for you to need support?

THE RIGHT HELP AT THE RIGHT TIME

Homework exercises are of the most use to you when you use them frankly and honestly. Sometimes this may mean thinking and writing about a subject that may be difficult, because it requires a frank appraisal of yourself or someone else.

Sometimes, being honest about your feelings may feel like being critical of others, or even ungrateful, but it isn't—it's just describing the way you feel. Your job in this homework exercise, as in all others, is to be totally honest about your feelings.

1. Is the sort of support you're receiving the sort of support you need or want?

_____

_____

_____

_____

2. What kind of support do you most need?

_____

_____

_____

_____

3. What kind of support do you least want?

_____

_____

_____

_____

4. Describe your three greatest practical needs at this time:

_____

_____

_____

5. Now name your three greatest emotional needs:

_____

_____

_____

6. Are the people in your support system accurately recognizing your needs?

_____

_____

_____

_____

7. What do you need to do in order to get the sort of support you really want?

_____

_____

_____

_____

8. Are you doing what you need to get your needs for support met?

_____

_____

_____

_____

Remember to bring the completed worksheet to your next appointment.

RECOGNIZING SUPPORT

GOALS OF THE EXERCISE

People sometimes look for support in the wrong places, without recognizing the types and sources of support actually available. This exercise will help clients think about what types of support are out there, who is available for support, and how they can begin to match the sorts of help needed with the sorts of help available.

TYPES OF SITUATIONS FOR WHICH THIS EXERCISE MAY BE MOST USEFUL

This exercise will help clients recognize the types of help and support needed, and where to find such support. Exercises of this sort can help clients who have difficulty accepting or seeking help recognize the importance of help and the necessity of getting the right type of help. The exercise will help clients distinguish between help that is naturally and easily available to them and help that must be sought out or "drafted."

SUGGESTIONS FOR PROCESSING THIS EXERCISE WITH CLIENTS

- Do you see a difference between help and support? Is it difficult to ask for either?

- Do you ever worry that your support will dry up over time, or that people will expect you to get over your grief?

- Do you use your support appropriately? Do you underuse support, do you take your support for granted, or do you ever wonder if you depend too much on your support?

- Did you place your therapist in the inner or outer circle of your natural support system? Is there a way to use your therapist more effectively for support?

- Do you need to more actively seek out support? If so, natural or drafted, or both types?

RECOGNIZING SUPPORT

1. What sorts of people are available to you for support? Your *natural* support group typically includes those people in your daily life—those in your inner circle who know you the best, and will provide the strongest and most immediate response to your grief. The support provided by people in your outer circle is likely to be more limited, less intense, and relatively short-lived.

   Usually you have to seek out *drafted* support—help outside of your natural system. In fact, you already have drafted support in your therapist or grief counselor, and may also have other such support in your life. If these types of supporters are presently in your life, think of them as part of your natural support system, in either the inner or outer circle.

2. Check off the *types* of support available to you (but not individuals). Add other sources of support in the spaces provided.

Natural Support

Type of Support	Inner Circle	Outer Circle	Drafted Support
Clergy	____	____	____
Close friends	____	____	____
Coworkers	____	____	____
Counseling support group	____	____	____
Counselor/therapist	____	____	____
Family physician	____	____	____
Family therapist	____	____	____
Home health	____	____	____
Home help	____	____	____
Immediate family	____	____	____
In-laws	____	____	____
Neighbors	____	____	____
School officials (for parents)	____	____	____

School officials (for students)   ____   ____   ____

Teachers   ____   ____   ____

Work supervisor   ____   ____   ____

_____   ____   ____   ____

_____   ____   ____   ____

_____   ____   ____   ____

_____   ____   ____   ____

_____   ____   ____   ____

3. You just checked off groups of people who are available to you for support. Now think of five people from within your natural support group you can turn to for support and help. Write their names in the spaces provided.

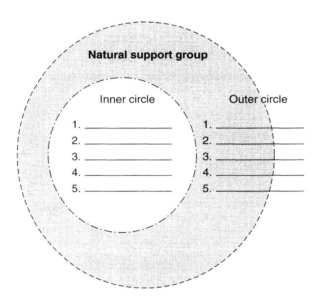

4. Think about the kinds of needs you named in the previous homework exercise ("The Right Help at the Right Time"). Can any of the people named above provide you with the kind of help or support you've identified?

_____

_____

_____

_____

5. Do these people know the kind of support you need from them?

6. At this point in your grief, do you think you're going to have to draft some additional support and assistance? If so, what kind of support will you need?

Remember to bring the completed worksheet to your next appointment.

CHECKPOINT: SUPPORT

GOALS OF THE EXERCISE

The final exercise in the section consolidates learning by seeking a recap from the client and focusing on what prevents the client from seeking or accepting help.

TYPES OF SITUATIONS FOR WHICH THIS EXERCISE MAY BE MOST USEFUL

Each exercise in the section prompts clients to consider not only their needs for help, but their ability and willingness to seek out, ask for, and accept help. The exercise is most important and most useful in situations where you want clients to really examine their patterns of seeking or rejecting help.

SUGGESTIONS FOR PROCESSING THIS EXERCISE WITH CLIENTS

- Do you feel you have a pretty clear sense of the kind of support you need, the kind of support you have, and how to get support?

- What have you learned about your needs? What have you learned about the role of support in your life at this time?

- Are you active enough in seeking out support?

- Are you willing enough to accept support?

- Is it possible to become too dependent on support? Are you too dependent on support?

- Is it important to repeat this exercise again after some time has passed? In what ways do you think your needs for support and help will change over time?

CHECKPOINT: SUPPORT

1. How can you tell when you need support or help?

   _____

   _____

   _____

   _____

2. When you need support, do you seek it out?

   _____

   _____

   _____

   _____

3. When offered support, do you accept it?

   _____

   _____

   _____

   _____

4. Do you expect people to automatically know you need support, or do you think that you need to tell them you need support?

   _____

   _____

   _____

   _____

5. Name five things that interfere with your willingness to let people know you need support or help, or to accept it when it is offered:

_____

_____

_____

_____

_____

6. Whose help have you accepted, and why?

_____

_____

_____

_____

7. Whose help haven't you accepted, and why not?

_____

_____

_____

_____

8. Write a few words on the place of support and help in your life right now.

_____

_____

_____

_____

Remember to bring the completed worksheet to your next appointment.

Section V

SHARING

This section includes four exercises. The grief work addressed in this section revolves around the need to share thoughts and feelings with others; the exercises describe sharing as a special form of support, elaborating on the importance and value of sharing as a mutual process with others in one's community.

PURPOSE

This section helps clients to recognize the act of sharing as a special form of getting *and* giving support.

TYPES OF SITUATIONS FOR WHICH THIS INFORMATION MAY BE MOST USEFUL

During difficult periods, some clients may find it difficult to share their feelings comfortably, for many different reasons. In some cases, people may feel too vulnerable to share; in others, they may wonder if anyone really wants to hear about their feelings, needs, and fears. In still other cases, often based on personality and even gender, people may not be prone to sharing. In all cases, and for whatever the reason, without sharing clients risk becoming isolated and cut off emotionally, unable to express their grief or get the help and support they need to work through their grief. And in some cases, clients may be unable to provide others with the help and sharing *they* need to deal with grief.

SHARING

Because the experience of grief can be so dislocating, it's perhaps most difficult when your loss isn't shared with others. A sense of being connected and belonging to a community is very important as you move through the grieving process.

In the previous section, you focused on support—its meaning, where to get it, and how to best use it. In this section, the focus is on sharing—but sharing is simply another face of support, and support and sharing both require and involve community:

- Support implies *community*—a group of people to whom you can turn when you need help. When you share, you share with others in that same community.

- To get support you have to *share*—you're not likely to get support unless, in some way, you've shared your loss and your needs.

- Although support after bereavement is often one-way (usually, you *receive* support), both support and sharing can go in *either* direction—you can get support, or give it; you can share and be shared with. Support and sharing can flow in one direction, or flow mutually in both directions at the same time.

Perhaps this last aspect is the most critical—support and sharing can move only in one direction, or they can be *mutual* processes. You can give *and* take at the same time.

THE FACES OF SHARING

Like support, sharing serves different purposes at different times. Sharing can support and strengthen you in your bereavement, and it can also serve to link you with others. Sharing with others can relieve your feelings, and also allow you to distribute your load among others who can help carry you through this difficult time. Sharing allows you to talk and reminisce with others who also cared for your loved one. Perhaps as important, sharing allows others to share their bereavement with you—you are almost certainly not the only one affected deeply by this loss. Others may need your help, your comfort and consolation, and your support. Sharing allows you to use your support to get through a difficult time, and brings the community together.

THE FACES OF SHARING

GOALS OF THE EXERCISE

This short exercise helps clients think about their patterns of sharing, including what is difficult to share.

TYPES OF SITUATIONS FOR WHICH THIS EXERCISE MAY BE MOST USEFUL

This exercise can help clients better understand their patterns of and comfort with sharing, including what sorts of things they're willing and able to share, and with whom. As with all the exercises, the goal of this exercise and the others in the section is to help clients more freely share and connect with others. This exercise should have special value in situations in which clients tend to be isolated or feel unable to easily share with others.

SUGGESTIONS FOR PROCESSING THIS EXERCISE WITH CLIENTS

- Is there a pattern to the kind of sharing you do? Is there a pattern to the kind of sharing you don't do?
- What most motivates your willingness or need to share with others?
- Do you share enough? Are there things you ought to be sharing, but aren't?
- What are your greatest fears about sharing?
- Are there others who you should be sharing with? Who are they, and why should you be sharing more with them? Why aren't you sharing more with them?
- Do you allow others to share with you? Are there others who need to share more with you?

THE FACES OF SHARING

1. Check off all those ways of sharing that are typical for you:

   ____ Letting people know when I need emotional help

   ____ Being with others when I need some company

   ____ Being with others when they need some company

   ____ Letting others know about the problems I face in managing my daily tasks

   ____ Telling people about my practical worries, like financial stressors

   ____ Reminiscing with others and sharing my stories and memories

   ____ Reminiscing with others and sharing their stories and memories

   ____ Sharing special events and commemorations with others in my community

   ____ Sharing decisions and future plans

   ____ *Other:* _____

   ____ *Other:* _____

   ____ *Other:* _____

   ____ *Other:* _____

   In which three ways are you most likely to share with others?

   _____

   _____

   _____

2. What are the three most difficult things to share?

   _____

   _____

   _____

3. Do you share different things with different people?

_____

_____

_____

_____

4. Who do you most typically share your thoughts and feelings with?

_____

_____

_____

_____

Remember to bring the completed worksheet to your next appointment.

THE FACES OF YOUR COMMUNITY

GOALS OF THE EXERCISE

This exercise directs clients to think about their connections to their support communities.

TYPES OF SITUATIONS FOR WHICH THIS EXERCISE MAY BE MOST USEFUL

This exercise is designed to help clients think about limitations on their ability or willingness to share with others, and about ways in which they might be limiting their ability to share with others and allow others to share with them.

SUGGESTIONS FOR PROCESSING THIS EXERCISE WITH CLIENTS

- Does your community meet your needs—do you need to think about expanding your community's ability to meet your needs? How can you do this?

- Do you need to take greater risks in sharing with others? What most restrains you from sharing more or sharing with more people?

- Can you take a risk by sharing more? What might you gain, and what do you fear you might risk by sharing more?

- Can you take a risk by sharing with someone you might not normally share with? What might you gain, and what might you risk by sharing with this person?

- Who needs to share with you, and what sort of things? Are you tuned in to the kind of help that others may need from you?

THE FACES OF YOUR COMMUNITY

1. Who's in your community? Who can you share with?

   _____

   _____

   _____

   _____

2. Of these people, who do you most feel comfortable sharing with?

   _____

   _____

   _____

   _____

3. Do you share similar things with each person, or different things?

   _____

   _____

   _____

   _____

4. How do you decide who you can and can't share with, or what you can share?

   _____

   _____

   _____

   _____

5. Does your community meet all, or just some, of your needs?

_____

_____

_____

_____

6. What would it be like to risk sharing with someone you normally don't share with?

_____

_____

_____

_____

7. Are there others in your community who are expressing their own deep grief for this loss?

_____

_____

_____

_____

8. What connection do you feel with others in your community whose grief is similar to your own?

_____

_____

_____

_____

9. Do you allow others to express and share their thoughts, feelings, and needs with you?

_____

_____

_____

_____

Remember to bring the completed worksheet to your next appointment.

THE GIFT OF SHARING

GOALS OF THE EXERCISE

This exercise draws attention to what things are the most important to share, and to those with whom the client shares important feelings and decisions. The exercise also helps clients think about who might need to be sharing their own thoughts and feelings with them.

TYPES OF SITUATIONS FOR WHICH THIS EXERCISE MAY BE MOST USEFUL

This exercise is designed to expand clients' senses both of what they have and are able to share with others, *and* of what they allow others to share with them.

SUGGESTIONS FOR PROCESSING THIS EXERCISE WITH CLIENTS

- Have you shared enough with others? Has sharing helped?
- Do you need to share more, or in different ways?
- Do you need to be more aware of the sort of support others may need from you?
- Do you need to reach out to people who may need you? Is it, or will it be, difficult to meet the needs of others?

THE GIFT OF SHARING

1. What have you shared about your loss, needs, or decisions? With whom?

_____

_____

_____

_____

2. What are the *most* important things for you to share?

_____

_____

_____

_____

3. Have you shared these things? If you have, was it useful, and do you need to share more? If you haven't been able to share, what's getting in the way?

_____

_____

_____

_____

4. Who shares with you?

_____

_____

_____

_____

5. What sort of things are shared with you?

_____

_____

_____

_____

6. Who needs to share with you? Who needs your support, and in what ways?

_____

_____

_____

_____

7. Are you pretty well tuned in to the needs of others?

_____

_____

_____

_____

8. If you've been able to meet their needs, has it helped you to help them?

_____

_____

_____

_____

9. Have you shared enough?

_____

_____

_____

_____

10. What more do you need to share, and with whom?

_____

_____

_____

_____

Remember to bring the completed worksheet to your next appointment.

CHECKPOINT: SHARING

GOALS OF THE EXERCISE

This last exercise in the section asks clients to think about whether they need to expand their community to ensure that it fits their needs, and if so, how.

TYPES OF SITUATIONS FOR WHICH THIS EXERCISE MAY BE MOST USEFUL

This exercise urges clients to think about their support communities and find ways to expand them in order to meet more of their own needs, and also to put something back into their support communities so that sharing is as much as possible a mutual process.

SUGGESTIONS FOR PROCESSING THIS EXERCISE WITH CLIENTS

- What are the limits of self-expression through individual therapy? In what ways do you need to directly communicate and share with others in your community?

- Are there parts of your therapy and what you're learning about yourself and your needs that you can share with someone else? Who might that person or those people be, and why would you choose them?

- Do you need to be especially aware of anything in your community, about your own or anyone else's needs?

CHECKPOINT: SHARING

1. How do you see your present community?

   _____

   _____

   _____

   _____

2. Which of your needs are outside of the scope of your present community? Why?

   _____

   _____

   _____

   _____

3. Do you need to expand your community, or is it meeting your needs as it is?

   _____

   _____

   _____

   _____

4. What four things could you do to expand your community?

   _____

   _____

   _____

   _____

5. What would be one supportive or sharing activity that would be of help to your community?

_____

_____

_____

_____

Remember to bring the completed worksheet to your next appointment.

Section VI

UNDERSTANDING FEELINGS

The goals of the six homework exercises in this section are to help clients learn to recognize and become aware of their feelings, and then understand some of the root causes. However, although they are geared toward grief and loss, the exercises in this and the next section are, in many ways, relatively generic—they address problems of experiencing and managing emotions under any circumstances.

PURPOSE

This section helps clients to understand that they *will* have painful feelings, and describes the normalcy of feelings that come and go during times of grief. This perspective also notes the importance of learning to accept and manage feelings during this period of grief, rather than finding ways to avoid or numb out feelings.

TYPES OF SITUATIONS FOR WHICH THIS INFORMATION MAY BE MOST USEFUL

In many ways, this section is generic and can work well for clients who have difficulty understanding or accepting their feelings under any circumstances. In particular, this material is of importance to clients who are experiencing difficulty with their emotions during their bereavement, or are feeling confused or overwhelmed.

UNDERSTANDING FEELINGS

There is nothing more natural than feelings, and you've no doubt been flooded with feelings since your loss, frequently without any conscious thought. If they've been especially difficult to bear, you may well have wanted to be rid of your feelings. But by now, you know that no matter how much you write about your feelings, you still have them. Expressing feelings doesn't evacuate them—it doesn't rid you of the feelings, but may help you to bear and manage them, and may even lighten the toll your feelings may be taking on you.

BECOMING AWARE OF FEELINGS

Before you can express a feeling, you first have to realize you're *having* a feeling. And, to prevent yourself from being swept away by a powerful feeling, you have to think about it and understand it. Recognizing that you have a feeling is the *buffer*—the bridge—between emotion and thought.

Since your loss, you've been trying to manage, and eventually overcome, unpleasant and difficult feelings. Your ability to recognize and understand your feelings is crucial to this goal. This process of recognizing and thinking about your feelings is a step toward emotional regulation—not the *stopping* of your feelings, but a way to express them positively, instead of acting them out inappropriately. Simply put, coping with a feeling doesn't mean you don't feel an emotion—it does mean you don't let it overwhelm you.

YOUR FEELINGS

GOALS OF THE EXERCISE

This exercise is simply a feelings checklist that clients can use repeatedly to zero in on how they're feeling and why. The intention is to tune clients in to their feelings.

TYPES OF SITUATIONS FOR WHICH THIS EXERCISE MAY BE MOST USEFUL

This exercise will help clients recognize how they're feeling, and why. It provides a check-list of basic feelings, many of which clients will feel during their bereavement. This is an homework exercise that clients should use over and over as they learn to focus on their emotions and process them.

Clients should work on this exercise shortly before or after situations that are emotionally difficult for them, or when they find themselves feeling especially emotional.

SUGGESTIONS FOR PROCESSING THIS EXERCISE WITH CLIENTS

- Were you easily able to pick out feelings? If you've used this homework format more than once, is it getting easier to recognize your feelings?

- Do you understand why you feel the way you do? Is it important to understand how you feel?

- Do you want to be able to regulate your feelings? Does understanding your feelings help you to regulate them?

YOUR FEELINGS

Something as simple as stopping and thinking about how you're feeling at a difficult moment can be a very useful way to regulate and cope with that emotion.

This exercise will help you recognize how you're feeling, and why. It provides a checklist of very basic feelings, many of which you'll feel during your bereavement. This is an exercise you should repeat often as you learn to focus on your emotions and process them.

Work on this exercise shortly before or after a situation that may be emotional for you in some way or another, or when you find feelings washing over you. It's a simple way to help pick up and understand a feeling.

How am I feeling?   **Why am I feeling this way?**

_____ Afraid   _____

_____ Amused   _____

_____ Angry   _____

_____ Anxious   _____

_____ Ashamed   _____

_____ Bitter   _____

_____ Detached   _____

_____ Disappointed   _____

_____ Foolish   _____

_____ Guilty   _____

_____ Happy   _____

_____ Helpless   _____

_____ Hopeful   _____

_____ Hopeless   _____

_____ Ignored   _____

_____ Incapable   _____

_____ Irritated   _____

_____ Lonely   _____

_____ Numb   _____

_____ Overwhelmed _____

_____ Sad   _____

_____ Trapped   _____

_____ Vulnerable   _____

_____ Worthless   _____

_____ Yearning   _____

Describe the situation that led to this feelings or feelings:

_____

_____

_____

_____

Remember to bring the completed worksheet to your next appointment.

YOUR THOUGHTS ABOUT YOUR FEELINGS

GOALS OF THE EXERCISE

This exercise builds on the previous exercise, but allows greater analysis. The exercise should be used repeatedly to focus in on one feeling at a time.

TYPES OF SITUATIONS FOR WHICH THIS EXERCISE MAY BE MOST USEFUL

This exercise will help clients become more familiar and comfortable with their feelings, especially if used often. It is most appropriate for clients who easily become overwhelmed or lost in feelings, or for clients who want to better understand the causes of their feelings and learn to better manage them. Asking clients how they might want to handle this feeling again in the future offers the opportunity to use a cognitive-behavioral approach in grief work.

SUGGESTIONS FOR PROCESSING THIS EXERCISE WITH CLIENTS

*   Is it possible to have different feelings at the same time? How do you decide which is the predominant feeling?

*   Is it possible to have opposite feelings at the same time? How do you deal with the contradiction?

*   Have you learned more about this feeling? Was your feeling more complicated than you initially thought it was?

*   How will you manage this feeling again in the future?

*   If you've used this homework format more than once, are you learning more about your feelings? What are you learning?

*   Does understanding your feelings help you manage them?

YOUR THOUGHTS ABOUT YOUR FEELINGS

1. Think about the feelings you identified in the previous homework exercise ("Your Feelings"). Name these below; if you picked more than six, just pick the six most powerful feelings you checked off.

   _____   _____

   _____   _____

   _____   _____

2. Of these feelings, which two were predominant?

   _____   _____

3. For this exercise, pick just one of these feelings to focus on:

   _____

4. Describe in more detail how you felt.

   _____

   _____

   _____

   _____

5. What situation led to the feeling?

   _____

   _____

   _____

   _____

6. Do you understand why you felt that way?

_____

_____

_____

_____

7. How did you handle the feeling?

_____

_____

_____

_____

Sometimes, when people stop and think about what they're feeling, they realize they're feeling "sad" more than "mad," or "disappointed" more than "angry." What feeling did you pick? Looking back on the feeling you've just thought and written about, do you think you've described the right feeling?

8. Are you satisfied with the way you handled this feeling?

_____

_____

_____

_____

9. What changes might you make to better handle this feeling in the future?

_____

_____

_____

_____

10. Do you think it was important to have this feeling?

_____

_____

_____

_____

Remember to bring the completed worksheet to your next appointment.

HOW DO YOU FEEL RIGHT NOW?

GOALS OF THE EXERCISE

This exercise will help clients learn more about the relationship between feelings and moods, and identity and explore moods as they experience them. Again, this is an exercise to be used frequently.

TYPES OF SITUATIONS FOR WHICH THIS EXERCISE MAY BE MOST USEFUL

This exercise is most useful for clients whose emotions are labile and who experience rapid mood shifts or swings. The exercise should be completed during the onset of the mood, so that there is a way for your clients to express their feelings as experienced, put words to them, and later bring the words to therapy where the experience can be processed. The exercise can be repeated time and time again to explore not just single occurrences, but patterns of moods and emotions. However, not all moods are bad moods. Encourage your clients to use the exercise as they experience good moods also, which hopefully will happen with increasing frequency over time.

SUGGESTIONS FOR PROCESSING THIS EXERCISE WITH CLIENTS

- If this is an unpleasant mood, what can you do to avoid situations that contribute to this mood? If it is a pleasant mood, what sort of situations or relationships stimulate this mood and keep it alive?

- If you've completed this exercise more than once, do you have a clearer sense of your moods and what affects them?

- Have the types or frequency of your moods changed over time, since your loss? In what ways?

- Are your moods so long lasting or intense that they affect your ability to function? If they are, do you feel you need help with them?

HOW DO YOU FEEL RIGHT NOW?

Some feelings last a while, and are more like a *collection* of feelings, rather than a single emotion. These are *moods,* or a set of underlying feelings that color everything for you while in that mood. When people's feelings change quickly or their feelings isolate them from others, they're often described as *moody.*

As you move through your grief work, you'll no doubt experience many moods. The most useful time to write about a feeling is when you're having it, and the most useful time to think about a mood is when you're in it. *Complete the next exercise only when you're in the grip of a mood.* Look the exercise over now, but complete it only when you can write about a mood that you're actually experiencing at that moment. You may not *want* to write when in an emotionally difficult mood, but this is the challenge and discipline of therapeutic homework assignments.

But, of course, not all moods are bad—some moods are lighthearted and fun. These moods are important to write about also. As you move through your grief work, you'll experience more and more good moods.

1. What kind of mood are you in?

   _____

   _____

   _____

   _____

2. Describe your mood in a single word.

   _____

3. What are the main emotions in this mood?

   _____

   _____

   _____

   _____

4. Put this mood into words.

   This mood is . . . _____

   _____

   _____

   If this mood had a color, it would be . . . _____

   If this mood had texture, it would be . . . _____

   If this mood made a noise, it . . . _____

5. Describe your mood in words.

   I feel . . . _____

   _____

   _____

6. What brought this mood on?

   _____

   _____

   _____

   _____

7. How long have you been feeling this way?

   _____

   _____

   _____

   _____

8. Is this a familiar mood to you?

   _____

   _____

   _____

   _____

9. Is this mood so strong that it's interfering with your daily life?

_____

_____

_____

_____

Remember to bring the completed worksheet to your next appointment.

TRIGGERS

GOALS OF THE EXERCISE

Through this exercise, clients will be able to identify people, places, and things that evoke strong feelings in them, and will think about how to deal with these triggers.

TYPES OF SITUATIONS FOR WHICH THIS EXERCISE MAY BE MOST USEFUL

This exercise is especially useful for clients whose feelings are easily triggered by certain situations, people, landmarks, or other things that evoke difficult feelings and painful memories.

The questions asked in this exercise are too broad to be simply answered in a single piece of homework. Accordingly, the exercise should be used to help clients think about their triggers in general; alternatively, it can be used to hone in on a particular trigger (situation, person, place, or thing), or be used repeatedly to cover multiple triggers.

SUGGESTIONS FOR PROCESSING THIS EXERCISE WITH CLIENTS

- There are bound to be some triggering situations or people you can't avoid. Are there other ways to minimize their triggering effect on you?

- Are there situations or people that really bring out the best in you? Are there ways to connect more with them?

- Are there other kinds of triggers in your life? What are they?

TRIGGERS

When feelings can be tied to certain kinds of situations, you can do something about them. Knowing that being around family makes you feel safe and comfortable tells you that this is a good place to be—when you're feeling anxious, just being around your family can help. On the other hand, if you know that passing a certain landmark every day on your way to work brings back sad and depressing memories, you can change your route to work. Knowing your *triggers* allows you to take more control over your life.

Triggers are those things in your life that activate or arouse feelings and reactions. They can be people, sounds, smells, or situations—anything, in fact, that brings back memories or feelings. As people usually want to enjoy pleasant thoughts and feelings, it's only the things that trigger unpleasant memories and emotions that are to be avoided. Triggers that stimulate good feelings and nostalgia are to be embraced. Understanding your triggers can help you decide what to move toward and what to move away from on your healing journey.

This exercise will help you look at those things that trigger unpleasant or distressing feelings.

1. Are there certain types of situations that predictably trigger feelings in you?

   _____

   _____

   _____

   _____

2. Are there certain people who are triggers for you?

   _____

   _____

   _____

   _____

3. Are there things besides situations and people that are triggers for you—sights, smells, or sounds? Music, movies, or clothing?

_____

_____

_____

_____

4. What emotions or thoughts do these things trigger?

_____

_____

_____

_____

5. Why do these things trigger these feelings and thoughts?

_____

_____

_____

_____

6. If these are the sorts of feelings you want to avoid, what can you do to avoid the triggers? What alternatives are there?

_____

_____

_____

_____

Remember to bring the completed worksheet to your next appointment.

WATCHING YOUR FEELINGS

GOALS OF THE EXERCISE

The goal of this exercise is to help clients tune in on feelings they haven't yet addressed in this section. In particular, this exercise will help clients sort through emotions and feelings that aren't always easy to understand or name, and thus help get to the heart or the meaning of the emotional difficulty. This exercise will also help clients to spot positive feelings, or those feelings that help rather than hinder grief-work recovery.

TYPES OF SITUATIONS FOR WHICH THIS EXERCISE MAY BE MOST USEFUL

In many cases, we treat emotions as simple constructs that can easily be recognized, named, and processed. In fact, much of the time emotions are more elusive, and are a composite or the result of other emotions. This exercise can be used repeatedly to help clients analyze complex emotions that are not easily recognized or named, derive meaning from the emotion, and learn to become more emotionally self-regulating in the process.

SUGGESTIONS FOR PROCESSING THIS EXERCISE WITH CLIENTS

• What have you learned about the way you deal with feelings?

• Are your feelings more complex and subtle than you realized? Have we been focusing too much on the obvious, surface emotions and not enough on emotions that are more difficult to spot and name?

• Is it helpful to use these homework exercises to delve into and understand your feelings in more detail?

• Do you think that understanding your feelings will help you deal with your grief? In what ways?

WATCHING YOUR FEELINGS

It's not always easy to put a name on feelings—emotions are often more complex than that. You may find that you've experienced feelings that have no simple name, or that are composites of several feelings. "Confusion," for instance, is really not a feeling, but more a mixture of feelings, or an inability to name a single feeling.

1. Give names to six other feelings (or mixes of feelings) that you've had, which haven't been otherwise named in other exercises in this section. Be inventive and call the emotions anything you like, but find a name that seems to aptly describe the feeling.

_____

_____

_____

_____

_____

_____

2. Describe one of these feelings in more detail.

_____

_____

_____

_____

3. Is it important to talk about any of these feelings in therapy or to write about them through homework exercises?

_____

_____

_____

_____

4. During your bereavement, you're experiencing a lot of feelings that are negative and that can interfere with your functioning. Are there feelings that you can *use* to help in your recovery and general sense of well-being?

_____

_____

_____

_____

5. What is it that's helpful about these feelings?

_____

_____

_____

_____

6. Is there any relationship between your difficult-to-deal-with feelings and your positive feelings?

_____

_____

_____

_____

7. How can your feelings, including the difficult and negative feelings, help you in your bereavement?

_____

_____

_____

_____

8. What can you learn from your feelings?

_____

_____

_____

_____

Remember to bring the completed worksheet to your next appointment.

OWNING YOUR FEELINGS

GOALS OF THE EXERCISE

The final and very brief (two-question) exercise in this section will help clients think about whether they displace their emotions onto others, and how they might better deal with their feelings. Unlike most exercises in *Grief Counseling Homework Planner,* this exercise provides a description of displacement so that clients are better equipped to recognize and express their emotions honestly and without displacement.

TYPES OF SITUATIONS FOR WHICH THIS EXERCISE MAY BE MOST USEFUL

Some clients simply push their feelings onto other people or things, and find any opportunity to dump their feelings in this way. This is something that most people do under the best of circumstances. However, as part of the goal of grief work is to experience and appropriately express feelings, and we are especially concerned about poorly managed feelings, this exercise is most appropriate for clients who fail to recognize or experience the true source of their feelings by displacing them onto other people or things.

SUGGESTIONS FOR PROCESSING THIS EXERCISE WITH CLIENTS

- What have you learned about the way you deal with feelings?

- Do you displace your feelings onto others? If you didn't displace feelings, what might happen? Would it become more difficult to deal with your feelings, or easier?

- Do you think that understanding your feelings will help you deal with your grief? How?

- Do you think understanding your feelings will help you deal better with other people in your life? Who, and why?

OWNING YOUR FEELINGS

After a bad day at work you might feel annoyed at the first pedestrian who doesn't cross the road fast enough, or you might find yourself getting easily irritated at something you hear on the news. You might go home and yell at the kids—even though you may realize it's not really the kids you're mad at. On the other hand, when things are going well, you might find that everything looks good. These are examples of *displaced* feelings—feelings about one thing that get placed on another.

At this time in your life—when you're experiencing many difficult moments, feelings, and moods—it's easy to displace your feelings onto someone or something else. Displacement is easiest to do when you're not conscious of doing it—and it begins when you're not even aware you're having a feeling, or you're trying to squash the feeling and pretend it's not there. But even if you don't recognize the feeling, or are ignoring it, it doesn't go away. Instead, the feeling may get expressed—usually inappropriately—through displacement. You let off steam in the wrong way, and probably at the wrong person.

It would be better to express your feelings—your fears, your anger, your disappointment—directly. To cry; to yell; to say how angry, sad, or scared you are, without losing sight of exactly what it *is* you're sad, upset, or frightened about. Displacing your feelings onto others—*dumping*—is not fair to them, and keeps you from dealing directly with the real source of your feelings.

As you complete the work in this section, it's important that you be in touch with your feelings and how you express them. Feelings are like weather vanes—they don't explain the weather, but they directly show you the direction and intensity of the wind. Feelings are the weather vane of your emotions—they don't necessarily offer insight into *why* you might be feeling emotional, but they are the direct line inside. If you stay in touch with your feelings, you'll have an important gauge to your emotional health that can help you control your emotions, rather than letting your emotions control you.

1. Do you displace your feelings? Onto whom, or what?

   _____

   _____

   _____

   _____

2. Do you need to find healthier or more appropriate ways to express feelings?

_____

_____

_____

_____

Remember to bring the completed worksheet to your next appointment.

Section VII

COPING WITH FEELINGS

Like every other section in the book, this section can certainly be used out of sequence, but it is designed to build on Section 6. This section includes four exercises that focus on managing feelings through the development of healthy coping mechanisms, and it describes certain styles of coping as self-destructive or self-defeating. The section also links emotions to behaviors, describing both positive and negative cycles of feelings and behaviors. This section signals the start of Stage 2 grief work. Clients should ideally be near or in the second stage of their grief work for this section to be most useful.

For clients who are doing generally well, this will be a straightforward section, allowing an introspective look at coping styles and activities. For clients who are not coping well, or are using unhealthy or self defeating means to cope, the section will prove more challenging and crucial.

PURPOSE

This information describes the meaning of coping and distinguishes between healthy, appropriate coping and unhealthy coping.

TYPES OF SITUATIONS FOR WHICH THIS INFORMATION MAY BE MOST USEFUL

Some people will deal with and work their way through grief without special problems. Others will fall into poor and unhealthy behavioral patterns in an attempt to cope with the situation and their feelings, or will fall back into previous or background patterns of coping that are ineffective or, worse, self-defeating, self-destructive, or inappropriate in some other significant way.

This information and these exercises, like the work in the previous section, may be used to help clients cope with any situation laden with emotions. In the context of grief work, the exercises in this section are especially pertinent for those who seem unable to find effective and appropriate ways to cope with their grief and other feelings resulting from their sense of loss.

COPING WITH FEELINGS

There are many ways to describe *coping*—to contend with; to endure, handle, manage, or survive; to struggle with—but, in the final analysis, to *cope* means to deal with a situation. As you work through your grief, you'll face many things with which you'll have to contend, but most of all you'll have to find ways to cope with your own feelings.

Coping with your feelings in healthy ways helps. Trying to cope in unhealthy ways invariably doesn't help—the problem, feeling, or situation still remains, and chances are you're worse off than when you began.

HEALTHY AND UNHEALTHY COPING

Emotions are the things you feel, while your behaviors are the things you do. Your feelings affect your behaviors, and sometimes shape them. Coping is what you do to handle your feelings so they don't overwhelm you. When you act out your feelings in ways that are self-destructive or self-defeating—such as not taking care of yourself, leaving responsibilities unfilled, or turning to substance abuse—you are demonstrating poor coping skills.

People seek ways to cope when their feelings become overwhelming. The more intense the feeling, the more you need to cope with it—feelings become like an underground pressure that forces action. Sometimes, the coping method is healthy—you cope with feelings by expressing them effectively, and succeed in taking the fury out of the emotion. It may still hurt or upset or bother you in some way, but its intensity is reduced, and you can move on with the daily events of your life. The feeling has fallen into the background, and you're able to put it into perspective, and either accept the situation leading to the feelings or figure out ways to resolve the problem.

Self-destructive or self-defeating behaviors are also attempts to cope with a feeling—the difference is that these are neither healthy nor effective ways of dealing with feelings. The goal, of course, is to help you develop healthy ways to cope with and manage your feelings in ways that help, not hurt or hinder.

HOW DO YOU COPE?

GOALS OF THE EXERCISE

This exercise begins a preliminary exploration of coping styles, including a spotlight on self-destructive, self-defeating, and healthy styles.

TYPES OF SITUATIONS FOR WHICH THIS EXERCISE MAY BE MOST USEFUL

This exercise will be useful for most clients, especially in helping clients to spot their coping styles, and most particularly if they use unhealthy or self-destructive coping mechanisms.

SUGGESTIONS FOR PROCESSING THIS EXERCISE WITH CLIENTS

- What most prevents you from coping with a feeling or situation? What most helps?

- Do you use only healthy coping mechanisms, or are some of your coping activities unhealthy or even self-destructive?

- Do unhealthy or self-destructive coping styles actually help, or do they create new problems?

- Do you keep any of your coping mechanisms hidden from others? If so, why? Is it because they're unhealthy?

- Can you build on or develop new healthy coping activities and substitute them for unhealthy coping mechanisms?

HOW DO YOU COPE?

1. As of today, what are the most pressing things you have to cope with?

_____

_____

_____

_____

2. What are the greatest obstacles to overcoming these things?

_____

_____

_____

_____

3. In what healthy ways do you cope? Check off all that apply, and add your own.

____ Art   ____ Dance   ____ Exercise

____ Gardening   ____ Hobbies   ____ Listening to music

____ Meditation   ____ Movies   ____ Playing an instrument

____ Reading   ____ Sports   ____ Talking

____ Therapy   ____ Walking   ____ Writing

_____   _____

_____   _____

_____   _____

_____   _____

4. Do you ever behave *self-destructively?*

_____

_____

_____

_____

5. In what ways is your behavior *self-defeating?*

_____

_____

_____

_____

6. What is your healthiest coping mechanism?

_____

_____

_____

7. What is your unhealthiest coping mechanism?

_____

_____

_____

Remember to bring the completed worksheet to your next appointment.

WHAT YOU DO IS WHO YOU ARE

GOALS OF THE EXERCISE

This exercise connects behavior to feelings and tunes the client into a reflective analysis of personal behaviors.

TYPES OF SITUATIONS FOR WHICH THIS EXERCISE MAY BE MOST USEFUL

This is an especially useful exercise for clients who seem out of touch with their behaviors or are unable to recognize that their behaviors have negative effects upon themselves or others. The exercise will help clients more easily see themselves as others may see them, judged by their behavior, or notice recent behavioral changes in themselves.

SUGGESTIONS FOR PROCESSING THIS EXERCISE WITH CLIENTS

- People often judge you by your "outside" person—through your behavior. Is there a different "inside" person?

- Do you feel okay about your behavior? Are there changes you want—or need—to make?

- Can you give an example of a recent situation in which you later regretted your behavior, and *why* you experienced later regret?

- Do you feel okay about the way that people see you? Do you wish they could see something different? What would that be?

WHAT YOU DO IS WHO YOU ARE

1. Do you ever behave in ways you later regret?

   _____

   _____

   _____

   _____

2. Do you ever *not* behave in ways you later wish you had?

   _____

   _____

   _____

   _____

3. Check off only those words that most describe your behavior since your loss. Add other words that most describe your behavior

   ____ Aggressive   ____ Angry   ____ Caring   ____ Confused

   ____ Considerate   ____ Courageous   ____ Depressed   ____ Disagreeable

   ____ Distant   ____ Fearful   ____ Flexible   ____ Friendly

   ____ Insecure   ____ Manipulative   ____ Obsessive   ____ Outgoing

   ____ Rigid   ____ Sad   ____ Selfish   ____ Withdrawn

4. Has your behavior changed since your loss? In what ways?

   _____

   _____

   _____

   _____

5. What behaviors do you often use? Check off all that apply, and add your own.

   ____ Yelling   ____ Laughing   ____ Drinking

   ____ Withdrawing   ____ Walking   ____ Smoking

   ____ Using drugs   ____ Interacting with others   ____ Talking

6. On reflection, are these the sorts of behaviors you want to use, and to be seen as using?

_____

_____

_____

_____

7. What message are you giving other people through your behavior? Do you mean to give this message? If you do, why?

_____

_____

_____

_____

8. If your behavior has changed, why has it?

_____

_____

_____

_____

9. Is there more to you than your behavior? What would you like people to know about you that they can't tell by your behavior?

_____

_____

_____

_____

10. Are there changes you want to make in your behavior?

_____

_____

_____

_____

Remember to bring the completed worksheet to your next appointment.

ONE AT A TIME

GOALS OF THE EXERCISE

This exercise should be used repeatedly to express individual feelings. The exercise once again directs clients to link their feelings with their behaviors.

TYPES OF SITUATIONS FOR WHICH THIS EXERCISE MAY BE MOST USEFUL

This exercise is useful in helping clients connect their feelings directly to their behaviors, especially when their behaviors are unhelpful, self-defeating, or outright self-destructive.

SUGGESTIONS FOR PROCESSING THIS EXERCISE WITH CLIENTS

- Do you deal with this feeling well? Does it ever get the better of you?
- Are there many feelings that are difficult for you to deal with, or just one or two?
- What will happen in the long run if you don't learn to cope with this and similar feelings?
- In general, what helps the most in dealing with difficult feelings?

ONE AT A TIME

Use this exercise repeatedly to express one feeling at a time. Repeat the exercise to revisit the same feeling again, or use it to think about a different feeling. This is a free-form exercise, which provides little structure—in this type of exercise, you simply write whatever comes into your mind.

The feeling for this exercise: _____

1. Describe this feeling.

   _____

   _____

   _____

   _____

2. How does this feeling affect your behavior?

   _____

   _____

   _____

   _____

3. How do you usually deal with this feeling?

   _____

   _____

   _____

   _____

4. Are you able to successfully cope with this feeling?

_____

_____

_____

_____

5. How will you deal with this feeling in the long run?

_____

_____

_____

_____

6. How will you deal with this feeling the next time you experience it?

_____

_____

_____

_____

Remember to bring the completed worksheet to your next appointment.

CHECKPOINT: COPING

GOALS OF THE EXERCISE

This is a short exercise to review coping styles and behaviors.

TYPES OF SITUATIONS FOR WHICH THIS EXERCISE MAY BE MOST USEFUL

This exercise wraps up the section, generally reviewing coping skills and desired or necessary changes and improvements in coping style.

SUGGESTIONS FOR PROCESSING THIS EXERCISE WITH CLIENTS

- How honest are you being in your homework? Have you honestly been able to look at and discuss your coping mechanisms and activities, or do you feel unable to fully bring them out into the open?

- Are you having special difficulties in coping, or in changing your coping behaviors? Do you need help, from friends or a professional?

- How would you know if your coping methods were negative? What do your friends and family members think? Do you feel able to ask?

CHECKPOINT: COPING

1. What have you learned about your coping behaviors?

_____

_____

_____

_____

2. How do your coping behaviors work? Why do they work?

_____

_____

_____

_____

3. Which coping methods do you most typically choose?

_____

_____

_____

_____

4. Are your coping behaviors positive or negative?

_____

_____

_____

_____

5. How well are you coping?

_____

_____

_____

_____

6. In what ways would you like to improve your coping skills?

_____

_____

_____

_____

Remember to bring the completed worksheet to your next appointment.

Section VIII

FINDING MEANING

The work in this section involves the loss of meaning that a death can bring (deconstruction) and the reconstruction and building of new meaning that follows. This section centers on the underlying philosophical and spiritual issues that often accompany the death of a loved one. As the six homework exercises in this section are more meditative than practical, clients should have completed some of the homework exercises in earlier sections that build experience and confidence in homework writing.

PURPOSE

This phase of grief work addresses the sense of meaningless that clients may experience when an important person passes away, leaving them alone and vulnerable, feeling empty and without direction.

TYPES OF SITUATIONS FOR WHICH THIS INFORMATION MAY BE MOST USEFUL

This section is particularly important for clients who are experiencing a loss of meaning or are questioning the value and purpose of life. This does not mean that clients are feeling suicidal, but rather feeling empty and detached. The death of an important person has led to the experience of *deconstruction,* in which those things that underpin and make up one's life have been suddenly stripped away.

The work in this section addresses the loss of meaning and the erosion of beliefs often experienced by the bereaved, especially when faced with the death of a romantic partner, a child, or someone with whom the bereaved person clearly shared his or her life.

However, the goal at this point in grief work is not to dwell on those parts of your clients' lives that have been deconstructed. Instead, these exercises will help clients to explore and understand the ways in which their beliefs and faith may have been shaken and to build a platform on which to reconstruct and restore beliefs and meaning.

FINDING MEANING

Meaning is that thing in our lives that adds richness and depth. Meaning gives significance, and often provides purpose and direction. Without meaning, life can be empty.

Death takes away many things. It robs you of your loved one, and sometimes your hopes and beliefs also. It may be that your loved one was too young to die, or your life together was just beginning. Perhaps the death is unfair to the children who remain behind, or your loved one went through pain that seemed needless and unfair. There are many scenarios—and in many of them, the survivors may be left confused, unable to understand how this could have happened, or why. Often, the bereaved seek meaning from a death that seems to have none. A death that seems unfair or senseless can seriously challenge the philosophical, spiritual, or religious beliefs of even the most devout believers, and leave them with a sense of meaningless.

DECONSTRUCTION

The loss of an important person in your life can lead to a sense of *deconstruction*—the removal of the things that underpin and make up your life. Even though you may be past the initial shock of the death, you may be feeling the depths of your emotions, and a sense of deconstruction can heighten your sense of loss and despair even further. Here, the experience may be loss of meaning and the erosion of your beliefs—the things that underlie the practical realities of your daily life and on which your expectations are built.

It's easy to get stuck in any stage of the grief process and to emotionally move no further. In such a case, although you will inevitably move on with your life, you won't have found the resolution and peace that completed grief work can provide. Deconstruction is the disassembly of your life, and the deconstruction of meaning—if you get stuck here, although life will move on, you may have great difficulty believing in anything again, trusting in the permanence of relationships, or building a new life for yourself in which you trust that your work and emotional efforts will be worth it.

THE QUALITY OF LIFE

GOALS OF THE EXERCISE

This exercise focuses on the ways in which clients' lives have been changed due to their loss, and on the *quality* of those changes.

TYPES OF SITUATIONS FOR WHICH THIS EXERCISE MAY BE MOST USEFUL

This exercise allows clients to think about how things have changed—and, indeed, how *they* have changed—since the death. The exercise invites self-reflection and works to help clients consider the quality of change and, perhaps, emptiness.

SUGGESTIONS FOR PROCESSING THIS EXERCISE WITH CLIENTS

- Does the world seem like a different place? Have your beliefs about the world been questioned in some way by this loss?
- Do you feel as though your world has lost some meaning? If so, is this is a serious challenge to your sense of meaning and order in the world, or does it simply require some time to adjust?
- How have *you* changed as a result of the death?

THE QUALITY OF LIFE

You've experienced the death of someone important in your life. In previous homework exercises, you've thought and written about how that loss has affected you and your life. In many ways, these exercises have focused on emotional and practical changes—the concrete experiences of death. For the exercises in this section—which deal with *meaning*—think about how your loss has changed the way you feel about life. First, take a few moments to think about how your life has changed since the death of your loved one.

1. What has your life been like since the passing of your loved one?

_____

_____

_____

_____

2. What are the three most difficult things to accept about the death?

_____

_____

_____

3. What three changes has it been the most difficult to adjust to?

_____

_____

_____

4. Your loved one has been lost to you. What else has been lost from your life?

Here, think about the quality of your life.

_____

_____

_____

_____

5. Has something changed in how you see or feel about the world since the death?

_____

_____

_____

_____

Remember to bring the completed worksheet to your next appointment.

MEANING IN YOUR LIFE

GOALS OF THE EXERCISE

This exercise asks clients to think about underlying systems of belief that normally guide their lives, and how these have been affected by the death of the loved one.

TYPES OF SITUATIONS FOR WHICH THIS EXERCISE MAY BE MOST USEFUL

The death of someone close causes some to question the meaning of the death and the meaning of spiritual or religious beliefs; for some, death can lead to a crisis in faith. This brief exercise is well suited for people who hold some kind of religious or spiritual faith, and who may be questioning how this death fits with or challenges their faith in some way.

SUGGESTIONS FOR PROCESSING THIS EXERCISE WITH CLIENTS

• Do you normally think about your beliefs, or do they simply remain in the background of your life? Have you found yourself thinking more about your belief system since your loss?

• Have your beliefs helped you to understand and accept your loss, or has your loss shaken your sense of faith or your beliefs?

MEANING IN YOUR LIFE

1. Do you think of yourself as (*check all that apply*):

____ Philosophical   ____ Religious   ____ Spiritual

____ Other: _____

2. Briefly describe your answer to the preceding question.

I believe . . . _____

_____

_____

_____

_____

3. What sort of underlying philosophy or belief system helps guide you or shapes your behaviors?

_____

_____

_____

_____

4. Do you consider yourself to be someone of faith? What does faith mean to you?

_____

_____

_____

_____

5. How has your loss affected your faith, or the meaning you give to the world?

_____

_____

_____

_____

Remember to bring the completed worksheet to your next appointment.

THE INGREDIENTS OF MEANING

GOALS OF THE EXERCISE

The focus remains on the quality of meaning and on how clients find meaning in their lives.

TYPES OF SITUATIONS FOR WHICH THIS EXERCISE MAY BE MOST USEFUL

This exercise will help clients focus on those things in their lives, including their loved one, that gave and continue to give meaning to life, helping clients find continued meaning. An exercise like this is useful for clients who are questioning meaning. The last question has clients write freely and automatically, without lifting the pen from the paper. This is an important question for clients, as their ability—or inability—to write meaningfully may set the pace for therapeutic discussion.

SUGGESTIONS FOR PROCESSING THIS EXERCISE WITH CLIENTS

* Do you already have a belief system strong enough to provide you with the meaning you need? What do you need to do to strengthen your belief system?

* Can you find meaning in your current life? What must you do to find or renew meaning in your life?

* Is finding *meaning* the same as getting *answers*? Do you need answers, or is finding meaning enough?

* What did you learn about meaning in your life from the final question in the exercise? What does your answer tell you about yourself?

THE INGREDIENTS OF MEANING

1. In what way was your loved one an ingredient in your life that added depth and meaning?

   _____

   _____

   _____

   _____

2. Can you find guidance or meaning in your current beliefs?

   _____

   _____

   _____

   _____

3. Look around you. What other ingredients in your life continue to give you direction and meaning, and serve to shape and define your life? Check off all that apply, and add at least three other elements of your life that provide meaning.

   ____ Career   ____ Children   ____ Community involvement

   ____ Friends   ____ Hobbies   ____ Pets

   ____ Parents   ____ Religion   ____ Spouse

   Other: _____

   Other: _____

   Other: _____

4. In what ways do these things hold meaning for you?

   _____

   _____

   _____

   _____

5. What other things in your life contribute to its richness and depth? (Examples might be art, music, reading, nature, volunteer work, and social causes.)

_____

_____

_____

_____

6. What meaning resides in the tasks of your daily life, or in the special tasks that you may have taken on since the death?

_____

_____

_____

_____

The last question in this exercise is free form. Look back at what you've just written and think about it for a moment. Then complete the following sentence, without stopping. Follow your thoughts wherever they take you, without lifting your pen from the page.

7. *I derive meaning in my life . . .*

_____

_____

_____

_____

Remember to bring the completed worksheet to your next appointment.

PERSONAL MEANING

GOALS OF THE EXERCISE

This exercise helps clients build strength and gather meaning from the passing of a loved one. It asks clients to think about how this loss has contributed to their personal growth.

TYPES OF SITUATIONS FOR WHICH THIS EXERCISE MAY BE MOST USEFUL

This exercise focuses on deriving meaning from the death itself, and what the experience of death and loss has taught your client. If used at the right time, with a client who is ready to see the death as a transition of sorts in his or her own life, the exercise can provide a valuable means for building strength and deriving meaning.

SUGGESTIONS FOR PROCESSING THIS EXERCISE WITH CLIENTS

- Has this loss helped you to personally grow in some way? If it has, were you surprised to realize you've grown? If it hasn't, what do you think is holding back your ability to help yourself find personal meaning?

- What is it like to realize that you can grow, even through loss?

PERSONAL MEANING

1. How can memories of your loved one provide support as you seek meaning?

   _____

   _____

   _____

   _____

2. What would your loved one want for you at this time in you life? What advice or direction would he or she offer you at this time?

   _____

   _____

   _____

   _____

3. Are there any special lessons or meanings that you can draw from the death of your loved one?

   _____

   _____

   _____

   _____

4. What have you learned about life through this death?

   _____

   _____

   _____

   _____

5. What has your loss taught you about relationships?

_____

_____

_____

_____

6. What is the most important thing you've learned through your loss?

_____

_____

_____

_____

7. How has loss added meaning to your life? How have you grown as a person?

_____

_____

_____

_____

Remember to bring the completed worksheet to your next appointment.

FRAGMENTS OF MEANING

GOALS OF THE EXERCISE

In this exercise, clients make a collage from photographs and other found materials. The focus is on the use of images and ideas to capture and reflect meaning.

TYPES OF SITUATIONS FOR WHICH THIS EXERCISE MAY BE MOST USEFUL

This exercise is most useful for clients who are able to express themselves nonverbally or who have an artistic orientation. It is also useful for those clients who are willing to stretch themselves and think and express themselves without words. Finally, the exercise may be useful for clients who are unable to find words for self-expression easily. Although the exercise concludes with two questions, it is also important that the therapist be comfortable with interpretation and/or exploration through created images rather than words.

SUGGESTIONS FOR PROCESSING THIS EXERCISE WITH CLIENTS

- What was it like to simply create without words? Did the process of collage making succeed in expressing your feelings?

- Were you able to find meaning in the process of making the collage? Were you able to find meaning in the finished collage?

- Is collage making something you want to do again? Are there other forms of artwork that might help you express feelings and explore meaning?

FRAGMENTS OF MEANING

This homework exercise and the following one offer a different way to explore and discover meaning. For this exercise, you'll create a *collage*—a compilation of photographs, parts of photographs, words, and other materials that are arranged and pasted to create a new picture. Go through your collection of photographs, magazines, and books and cut out entire images or parts of photos and pictures, as well as words. Use only those pictures and words that remind you in some way of your loved one or your loss. *As you select and cut out your materials, don't think about the finished collage—pick each thing based only on how that particular thing attracts or affects you.* Once you've cut out and collected each piece you want to use, paste them together in the space provided, or on a separate sheet of paper if you prefer. If you use the space provided here, you'll obviously have to be conscious of size. Once you've completed the collage, take some time to look carefully at it and think about how it makes you feel. Then complete the exercise by answering the questions on the page following the collage space.

Create your collage in this space.

1. Look back at the collage you've just created. How does it make you feel?

   _____

   _____

   _____

   _____

2. What does your collage mean? Can you find words to describe its meaning?

   _____

   _____

   _____

   _____

Remember to bring the completed worksheet to your next appointment.

A FRIDGE POEM

GOALS OF THE EXERCISE

Following the theme of the previous exercise, clients will "build" a poem out of found words, then reflect on its meaning.

TYPES OF SITUATIONS FOR WHICH THIS EXERCISE MAY BE MOST USEFUL

This is another exercise that can benefit clients who are unable to find words or who are willing to find ways to express themselves without the spoken, or even written, word. The exercise will also help those who are unable to easily find their own words to express thoughts and feelings. Although the exercise uses words, they are random words—found words—that are combined to produce meaning for interpretation.

SUGGESTIONS FOR PROCESSING THIS EXERCISE WITH CLIENTS

- What's the difference between *making* meaning and *finding* meaning? Did you make meaning from the words you chose for your poem, or find it within them?

- Do you have to look for meaning to find it? How can you keep finding meaning?

- Is writing or finding poetry something that can help you recognize or express your feelings at this time in your life?

A FRIDGE POEM

It's possible to make meaning out of a jumble of bits and pieces. In completing your collage in the previous exercise, you did just that. As you take disconnected parts and connect them, you create meaning, through the process of connection. But it's only after you've built the connective links and created something new that you're able to look for the meaning within.

In this exercise, you're going to create a "fridge poem." The exercise is named for the magnetic fridge poetry kits that have become popular. These kits are made up of hundreds of individual words that are printed on magnets—you can create messages or poems on your refrigerator by arranging them in the desired order.

For this exercise you can buy a fridge poetry kit, or you can simply cut 100 words at random from any magazine. Whether you use a kit or cut out your own words, select 35 to 50 words after you've gathered them all together, and from these create a poem inspired by your loss. There are no other directions for this poem.

1. Once you've completed the poem, reproduce it here.

_____

_____

_____

_____

_____

_____

_____

2. Reread your poem. How does rereading it make you feel?

_____

_____

_____

_____

3. What meaning is there in this poem for you?

_____

_____

_____

_____

Remember to bring the completed worksheet to your next appointment.

Section IX

BIOGRAPHY

Every section in *Grief Counseling Homework Planner* is about relationships, but this section and the next one most clearly focus on the relationship between the client and the deceased. The five homework exercises in this section will help the client create a picture that captures and reflects back on the life of the deceased.

This section is probably most appropriate for clients who are moving from Stage 2 (emotional immersion and deconstruction) to Stage 3 (reclamation and reconciliation) in their grief work.

PURPOSE

This section helps clients to think not just about the relationship itself and what they've lost through the death, but about the *person* they've lost.

TYPES OF SITUATIONS FOR WHICH THIS INFORMATION MAY BE MOST USEFUL

This section will help clients remember and explore the details of the life of their loved one. The exercises in the section help clients bring memories and feelings to life.

BIOGRAPHY

In other sections, you've written about your loss, your relationship with others, the personal meaning of your loss, and other thoughts and feelings in reaction to the death of your loved one.

But in some ways, these things are all secondary to the fact that you had a relationship with a *person*. Although that relationship took on a life and direction of its own in many respects, it could never have existed without your loved one. As you work through your grief, you also have to take the time to explore that relationship and the other person in it—your loved one. The exercises in this section will help you think about and explore aspects of who that person was—the life and times of your loved one. Through these exercises, you will create a biography of your lost friend.

I WANT THE WORLD TO KNOW

GOALS OF THE EXERCISE

This exercise has the client write an obituary, and commit to paper the details of the death and of the life that has passed.

TYPES OF SITUATIONS FOR WHICH THIS EXERCISE MAY BE MOST USEFUL

Obituaries serve a genuine function—they express feelings, memorialize the deceased, bring to the forefront the record of that person's life, and share that life with all who read the obituary. This exercise, like the others in this section, is useful in helping to move clients into a reflective and accepting mode, from which they can consider sharing their ideas, memories, and feelings with the world at large, thereby both expressing themselves and moving on.

SUGGESTIONS FOR PROCESSING THIS EXERCISE WITH CLIENTS

- What was it like to commit to paper the details of your loved one's death—the name, dates, and other information? Was it difficult, or did it further help to relieve feelings for you?

- Did you feel satisfied with the obituary you wrote? Did it say and express the things you wanted it to?

- Is there more than one obituary to write for your loved one?

- Will the obituary be a "keeper"—something you keep private and never share—or will you consider submitting it to a local publication?

I WANT THE WORLD TO KNOW

- Think first about what you want to say in an obituary. What do you want other people to know about your loved one? Do you want to write about only the facts and details of your loved one's life, or do you want to present a more intimate view that tells others who the deceased was in your life and what your loved one meant to others?
- Look through obituaries in your local newspaper. Get a sense of how they read, the sorts of things people write about their losses, and how reading them makes you feel.
- Begin with the basics of any biography—dates, places, and other important details that record a life and death.

1. Name of your loved one: _____

2. Birth date: _____ Date of death: _____

3. Place of birth: _____

4. Place of death: _____

5. Other important details that should be recorded as part of this obituary. (This may include marriages, births, and achievements.)

   _____

   _____

   _____

   _____

6. Write the obituary.

   _____

   _____

   _____

   _____

Remember to bring the completed worksheet to your next appointment.

A 10-MINUTE BIOGRAPHY

GOALS OF THE EXERCISE

This exercise provides another format that can used over and over. In this case, the client will create a brief biography of the deceased, focusing on only one aspect of the deceased's life.

TYPES OF SITUATIONS FOR WHICH THIS EXERCISE MAY BE MOST USEFUL

Again, this exercise brings ideas and memories from the inside to the outside. The exercise allows clients to record the life story of the deceased; through the cathartic acts of writing, self-expression, and committing history to paper, it can help clients expel feelings that may be preventing them from more fully moving on and release other feelings that may otherwise remain bottled up.

SUGGESTIONS FOR PROCESSING THIS EXERCISE WITH CLIENTS

- Was it easy to write a biography, or was it difficult to find the material to write about? If it was difficult, why?

- Was it satisfying to write this brief biography? Will you later want to write a longer biography?

- Can you write another biography? Do you want to? What different aspect of your loved one's life would it focus on?

- What was it like writing about the life of your loved one? Was it gratifying, sad, or both? Did it bring relief or remind you of your grief? How would you describe the experience?

A 10-MINUTE BIOGRAPHY

1. Take a few minutes to think about how to write this biography, and what aspect of your loved one's life to focus on:

    ____ Entire life   ____ Career choices   ____ Family influences

    ____ Childhood history   ____ Adolescence   ____ Early adulthood

    ____ School years   ____ Relationships   ____ Shaping incidents

    ____ Other: _____

2. Spend the next 10 minutes writing a biography of your loved one's life from the perspective you've chosen.

_____

_____

_____

_____

_____

_____

_____

_____

_____

_____

_____

_____

_____

_____

_____

_____

_____

_____

_____

_____

_____

3. What does the biography you've written say about *you*—the way you feel, and the way you see your loved one, today?

_____

_____

_____

_____

4. What most influenced your choice of biography?

_____

_____

_____

_____

5. If you wrote another biography, would it be different? Would you focus on the same material, or would you choose another slice of your loved one's life?

_____

_____

_____

_____

Remember to bring the completed worksheet to your next appointment.

A QUICK SKETCH

GOALS OF THE EXERCISE

This is a character sketch of the deceased that mostly follows a structured homework format, using sentence starts that the client will complete.

TYPES OF SITUATIONS FOR WHICH THIS EXERCISE MAY BE MOST USEFUL

This exercise will help clients deal with mixed feelings about the loved one's character strengths and flaws. It will help clients remain honest, without falling into the potential trap of not being able to express themselves fully about the totality of their loved one's character.

As clients move further into these exercises, it will be important to help them express the truth. Not every biography, for instance, paints a pretty picture. The character sketch may reveal a loving spouse or an abusive one. There is an opportunity here to help clients express difficult and darker sides of their loved one's character and their relationship, as well as those lighter and fonder things that they may perhaps want to remember the most.

SUGGESTIONS FOR PROCESSING THIS EXERCISE WITH CLIENTS

* Was it difficult to think about your loved one in small character chunks? Was it easiest to think about the special qualities, or did your loved one's flaws come to mind first?

* Does the character sketch work—that is, does it present an accurate portrait of your loved one?

* Is your view of your loved one balanced? Do some aspects tend to stand out more clearly than others? Is this okay?

* Was it difficult to think and write about those aspects of your loved one's flaws or your relationship that troubled and bothered you? Did it feel disloyal to write about what bothered you?

A QUICK SKETCH

1. My loved one was . . .

_____

_____

_____

_____

2. The thing that was most special about my loved one was . . .

_____

_____

_____

_____

3. The thing that most bothered me about my loved one was . . .

_____

_____

_____

_____

4. My loved one's best qualities were . . .

_____

_____

_____

_____

5. My loved one's most obvious flaws were . . .

_____

_____

_____

_____

6. The most unusual or oddest thing about my loved one was . . .

_____

_____

_____

_____

7. Describe your loved one.

_____

_____

_____

_____

Remember to bring the completed worksheet to your next appointment.

AN IMPORTANT POSSESSION

GOALS OF THE EXERCISE

The client will think about the deceased indirectly, through examining a possession that was important to the deceased in life.

TYPES OF SITUATIONS FOR WHICH THIS EXERCISE MAY BE MOST USEFUL

Some things will always remind us of people we've lost. Sometimes these objects are cherished, and sometimes bittersweet; sometimes they're painful reminders that are difficult to see again, yet impossible to let go of. This exercise will help clients explore their loved one's life through a favorite or important possession, and also will increase their understanding of their loved one through the object.

There is a wonderful opportunity here, as is true for all of these exercises, for clients to be honest with themselves. For instance, although an important possession may well be a favored piece of clothing, or a book, or an award, the important object may equally well reflect a significant problem—for example, a bottle of alcohol, which may represent a substance-abuse problem. Perhaps the possession was even responsible for the loved one's death—for example, a pack of cigarettes. Perhaps it is an object or possession that somehow served to keep others out, including the client. Accordingly, for some clients this can be a very important exercise, and may even serve to indicate reassigning earlier exercises again, depending on what is revealed.

SUGGESTIONS FOR PROCESSING THIS EXERCISE WITH CLIENTS

- Were you surprised at how much or how little you knew about the possessions most prized by your loved one?

- Did you learn anything about your loved one by considering the value of this object to him or her?

- Does this item carry fond reminders for you? Does it leave bad feelings for you, and if this is the case, is this part of unfinished business?

AN IMPORTANT POSSESSION

Pick something that was one of your loved one's most prized possessions. It doesn't have to be something that your loved one treated in a special way, or proclaimed to be cherished— it can simply be something that was clearly important because of the way your loved one treated or used it, or the place it held in your loved one's life.

It might be an favorite chair or desk, a book, or a much-worn article of clothing. It could be an award or trophy, a painting, or a pen. It might even be the television remote control. Pick one favorite item, but whichever one you choose, it must an inanimate object (rather than a pet, for instance).

Through this favorite possession, explore the life of your loved one—why was this item so important, and what did this choice say about your loved one? It may even be true that the your loved one's favored possessions weren't flattering. But the idea in this exercise, as it is true for all these exercises, is to reflect upon and find ways through grief that are honest and direct. The aim is to remember and cope, not to idealize and make sacred.

1. Decide which prized objects were among the most important to your loved one. Imagine that in death, your loved one could have taken one of these possessions along. Which would it be?

   _____

   _____

2. If you're able, go and get that object now and place it in front of you. If it's too large to move, go to it. Look at it carefully. Study its shape, its texture, and its qualities. Think about what it meant to your loved one, and why. Before continuing, describe the object.

   _____

   _____

   _____

   _____

3. Why was this object so important to your loved one?

_____

_____

_____

_____

4. What does this prized possession say about your loved one?

_____

_____

_____

_____

5. Is there anything appealing to you about this possession? Does it have any extra meaning since your loss?

_____

_____

_____

_____

6. Of all the things that your loved one owned or that were important to your loved one, why did you pick this thing?

_____

_____

_____

_____

Remember to bring the completed worksheet to your next appointment.

CHECKPOINT: BIOGRAPHY

GOALS OF THE EXERCISE

This last exercise provides a way for the client to look back at the biographies gathered through the section and reflect on the feelings generated by writing about the deceased in this way.

TYPES OF SITUATIONS FOR WHICH THIS EXERCISE MAY BE MOST USEFUL

You may choose to have clients complete each of the exercises in this section just once, or several times. As the next two sections continue the theme of shared history and commemoration, by the time you assign this final exercise, you should feel comfortable that the client has exhaustively, appropriately, and honestly described and exorcized feelings and memories about the deceased loved one.

SUGGESTIONS FOR PROCESSING THIS EXERCISE WITH CLIENTS

- The work in your grief homework is largely internal. Do you need to be more *external,* sharing with others what you're writing, feeling, thinking, and learning? If you're already sharing, are you satisfied that you're sharing with the right people?

- Are there others who are sharing your loss who might benefit by doing their own grief work?

CHECKPOINT: BIOGRAPHY

1. What has been the most useful part of writing a biography of your loved one?

   _____

   _____

   _____

   _____

2. As you complete this section, what needs to be said about your loved one that hasn't already been said?

   _____

   _____

   _____

   _____

3. There are many biographies about your loved one. In this section you wrote just one. Are there other biographies of your loved one that you'd write? If so, outline one or two ideas here to return to later.

   _____

   _____

   _____

   _____

4. Are there people with whom you want to share what you've written here?

   _____

   _____

   _____

   _____

5. As you complete this section and its homework exercises, how do you feel?

_____

_____

_____

_____

Remember to bring the completed worksheet to your next appointment.

Section X

SHARED HISTORY

This section continues the theme of Section 9, further exploring the relationship between the client and the deceased loved one. Although each section touches on deeply personal issues, this section provides a way for the client to think and write about the history shared with the deceased. In many ways it is an especially intimate section, with each of the five exercises touching on the special and unique qualities of the relationship.

PURPOSE

This section will help clients recognize that their relationship with the deceased was—and is—special because of the bond, and that bonds form a history shared between two people.

TYPES OF SITUATIONS FOR WHICH THIS INFORMATION MAY BE MOST USEFUL

This section will be useful in helping clients consider and explore the intimacy in their relationship with their loved one, and the meaning and roots of that connection. This sort of work is useful for clients who want to process their relationship and its development over time, and is helpful for clients who feel a deep sense of loss and want to better understand why they experience such a loss (and perhaps better understand exactly what it is that they have lost). Exploring, reminiscing, and understanding shared history can be cathartic, soothing, enlightening, and empowering.

SHARED HISTORY

Just as there's a history behind every person, the same is true for every relationship. Your memories and feelings are about both your loved one (and what he or she meant to you) and your relationship.

Although there are many types of relationships between people, only a few signify a *connection* in which the relationship contains meaning for each of the people in it. These can probably be boiled down to the sorts of relationships that exist between parents and children, close family members, romantic partners, and friends. In relationships of this type, there's a sense of shared lives, and often linked paths and shared destinies. What affects one person in the relationship affects the other. This is true of the relationship you had with your loved one. This is why you grieve.

The togetherness in your relationship was an emotional connection, and it's this emotional bond that sealed your relationship. Many of the exercises you're working on are chronicles of your thoughts, feelings, and experiences since the death of your loved one. But, they're also records of your life together and that emotional bond. For this reason, it can be very important to think about, write about, and explore your shared history—the things that you did and experienced together, the things that helped seal the bond between you and that will live on in you.

OUR RELATIONSHIP

GOALS OF THE EXERCISE

Clients will think about and describe the nature of their relationship with the deceased loved one and those things that connected them to the deceased in life.

TYPES OF SITUATIONS FOR WHICH THIS EXERCISE MAY BE MOST USEFUL

In many ways, this exercise is most obviously designed for people who chose their relationships—romances and friendships, for instance. But it can also be used to help clients consider their relationships with family members, where relationships happen by default rather than by choice. Nevertheless, many people never grow close to other family members, and when they do there are usually clear and special reasons. This exercise aims to help clients understand what made the relationship special and what held them close to their loved one, no matter what the relationship.

SUGGESTIONS FOR PROCESSING THIS EXERCISE WITH CLIENTS

- Was it easy or difficult to describe what bonded you—what kept you together? Did you already know what connected you, or did this exercise help?

- Has thinking about your relationship and your bonds left you with unanswered questions? If so, what can you do to get answers?

- Some of the questions seemed obvious—for instance, where did you meet? But was it easy to answer these obvious questions, or did you find blanks in your memories?

- Are there important early memories you want to spend more time recalling or writing about?

- Are there important people in your life today with whom you should be spending time and building bonds?

OUR RELATIONSHIP

This homework exercise is generic. As you complete it, you'll answer each question in ways that fit your relationship. For instance, if you're writing about your parent, your answers will be very different than if you're writing about a loved one who was your romantic partner.

Nowhere is this more true or more obvious than in the questions that ask you about where, when, and how you met your loved one. Make your answers as meaningful as possible, even when they seem obvious.

1. Describe your relationship.

　　_____

　　_____

　　_____

　　_____

2. What bonded you and your loved one?

　　_____

　　_____

　　_____

　　_____

3. What was the most important part of your relationship?

　　_____

　　_____

　　_____

　　_____

4. What brought you and your loved one together?

_____
_____
_____
_____

5. What kept you together?

_____
_____
_____
_____

6. Where did you meet?

_____
_____
_____
_____

7. How did you meet?

_____
_____
_____
_____

8. Complete the following sentence start.

   Our relationship was . . . _____
_____
_____
_____

Remember to bring the completed worksheet to your next appointment.

I REMEMBER

GOALS OF THE EXERCISE

Relationships don't just happen, and people don't become close to one another for no reason. The goal of this exercise is to help clients recognize moments that were important in the early development of their relationship, and help them understand that memory as part of a shared history that brought them closer to their loved one.

TYPES OF SITUATIONS FOR WHICH THIS EXERCISE MAY BE MOST USEFUL

This is an exercise for clients to complete over and over. Like the other exercises in this section, it can help clients more deeply understand their relationship and, in many cases, fondly recall and reminisce about important moments and turning points.

SUGGESTIONS FOR PROCESSING THIS EXERCISE WITH CLIENTS

- Is remembering important moments a pleasant or painful experience? Either way, why?

- Were all the important moments in your relationship pleasant experiences, or did some important moments turn on difficult events and circumstances?

- How did these important moments contribute to your relationship? How did they bind you to one another?

- How can your memories of important moments help sustain you in your life now?

- How are important moments and memories being built right now with other people in your life, and do you notice them as they occur?

I REMEMBER

This is an exercise to complete over and over. Pick just one important memory—but then think about other important memories that you may want to write about, and complete this exercise again—and again.

1. Recall one important memory of your early relationship.

_____

_____

_____

_____

2. Why is this an important memory?

_____

_____

_____

_____

3. How did this memory help bond you and your loved one?

_____

_____

_____

_____

4. How can you keep this memory alive and fresh?

_____

_____

_____

_____

Remember to bring the completed worksheet to your next appointment.

AN IMPORTANT DAY

GOALS OF THE EXERCISE

In this exercise, clients recall a significant and meaningful day in the history they shared with their loved one. The exercise encourages clients to think about important days that were good, as well as those that were bad.

TYPES OF SITUATIONS FOR WHICH THIS EXERCISE MAY BE MOST USEFUL

This exercise will help clients to more deeply understand their relationship and those shared experiences that made—and continue to make—the relationship important. The exercise is as much based on difficult or bad experiences as on good experiences; both count in the formation of lasting relationships, and often both need to be explored in grief work as clients deepen their understanding of both the relationship itself and the grief they are experiencing.

SUGGESTIONS FOR PROCESSING THIS EXERCISE WITH CLIENTS

- What was it like to recall this day? How did it leave you feeling?

- Is there a lesson to be learned from this day?

- Is it important to remember these days? Will you write about the other special days in your shared history?

- Was your relationship forged out of only positive experiences, or difficult experiences as well? Were some of the difficult experiences the result of tension *between* the two of you?

- Are there people in your life today with whom you should count every day as special?

AN IMPORTANT DAY

Think of days that stand out in your memory, either because you were with your loved one on that day or because your loved one shared this day with you in some other way. The day can be important for any number of reasons: It could be a fun day, or an awful one. It could be a milestone for one or both of you or for another member of your shared family, or it could be a milestone day in your relationship. Or it could be a day that you spent together that simply stands out because of the weather, or where you happened to be.

The day could be momentous, or just a fast-food meal together. It doesn't matter if it's a memory of a good day or a difficult time. What counts here is that the day has significance for some reason in your shared history.

1. List at least six important good days.

_____

_____

_____

_____

_____

_____

_____

_____

_____

2. List at least six important bad days.

_____

_____

_____

_____

_____

_____

_____

_____

_____

3. Pick one of these days—good or bad—as the focus of this homework exercise. (You can repeat the exercise again for each of the other days on your list.)

_____

4. Describe this important day.

_____

_____

_____

_____

5. Complete the following sentence starts.
   I chose to write about this day because . . .

_____

_____

_____

_____

This day is important in our history because . . .

_____

_____

_____

_____

The most important thing about this day is . . .

_____

_____

_____

_____

As I think of this day, it makes me feel . . .

_____

_____

_____

_____

As I relive this day now, I realize that . . .

_____

_____

_____

_____

Remember to bring the completed worksheet to your next appointment.

LIFE MARKERS

GOALS OF THE EXERCISE

Continuing to focus on the development of the relationship and its bonds, this exercise has the client think about milestones—significant events, anniversaries, and other landmarks—in the life of the relationship.

TYPES OF SITUATIONS FOR WHICH THIS EXERCISE MAY BE MOST USEFUL

Relationships often turn on important moments; when people look back, they can recognize these as markers of change or the development of a new turn in the relationship. These exercises will help clients to think back on those moments, or markers, on which the relationship was built and evolved. The exercise will help clients deepen their understanding of their relationship with the loved one.

SUGGESTIONS FOR PROCESSING THIS EXERCISE WITH CLIENTS

- What would your relationship have been like without milestones, anniversaries, and other landmarks? Is it possible to have a meaningful relationship without shared landmarks?

- Can you continue to celebrate important milestones and anniversaries, even though your loved one is deceased?

- Did all markers signal the beginning of positive events in your relationship? Did some set into motion difficult events or changes? What was the *last* important life marker in your relationship before the death of your loved one?

LIFE MARKERS

Think about those special days that were landmarks in your relationship. First think of three milestone events—days or times that you look back upon as turning points in your relationship or in the history that you shared with your loved one.

Then consider three anniversaries—days that marked a moment when something special happened that you commemorated on a regular basis in your relationship from that day on.

1. *Milestones.*   Why were these days significant, and what made them milestones for each of you?

   • Milestone: _____ Date: _____
     Significance: _____

     This milestone is important to me because . . .

     _____

     _____

     _____

     _____

     This milestone was important to my loved one because . . .

     _____

     _____

     _____

     _____

   • Milestone: _____ Date: _____
     Significance: _____

     This milestone is important to me because . . .

     _____

     _____

     _____

     _____

This milestone was important to my loved one because . . .

_____

_____

_____

_____

- Milestone: _____ Date: _____
  Significance: _____

  This milestone is important to me because . . .

  _____

  _____

  _____

  _____

  This milestone was important to my loved one because . . .

  _____

  _____

  _____

  _____

2. _Anniversaries._ What did these anniversaries commemorate, and why?

   - Anniversary: _____
     Date: _____ Celebrating _____ years

     This anniversary was important to us because . . .

     _____

     _____

     _____

     _____

     In our relationship, this anniversary meant . . .

     _____

     _____

     _____

     _____

- Anniversary: _____

  Date: _____ Celebrating _____ years

  This anniversary was important to us because . . .

  _____

  _____

  _____

  _____

  In our relationship, this anniversary meant . . .

  _____

  _____

  _____

  _____

- Anniversary: _____

  Date: _____ Celebrating _____ years

  This anniversary was important to us because . . .

  _____

  _____

  _____

  _____

  In our relationship, this anniversary meant . . .

  _____

  _____

  _____

  _____

3. Are there other important landmarks, turning points, or dates in your shared history?

   _____

   _____

   _____

   _____

4. How did landmarks such as these help build and seal your relationship?

_____

_____

_____

_____

Remember to bring the completed worksheet to your next appointment.

I'LL NEVER FORGET

GOALS OF THE EXERCISE

The final exercise in the section aims to encourage sheer reminiscence. Through a series of sentence starts, the exercise allows for completely open-ended answers, directing the client into a free-thinking mode about the relationship.

TYPES OF SITUATIONS FOR WHICH THIS EXERCISE MAY BE MOST USEFUL

This exercise simply allows clients to recall moments in their relationship that can prompt further exploration in therapy sessions. The exercise can be used at difficult times, and can help clients get unstuck or get in touch with ideas they want to bring into therapy.

SUGGESTIONS FOR PROCESSING THIS EXERCISE WITH CLIENTS

- Does your relationship live on in your memory? Have you found that your relationship still lives inside you?

- Who else is part of your shared history—family or friends? Can you keep drawing support from these other people? Do they need to keep drawing support from you?

I'LL NEVER FORGET

1. I'll never forget when we . . .

_____

_____

_____

_____

2. I'll never forget when you . . .

_____

_____

_____

_____

3. I'll never forget when we first . . .

_____

_____

_____

_____

4. I'll never forget . . .

_____

_____

_____

_____

5. I'll never forget . . .

_____

_____

_____

_____

6. I'll never forget . . .

_____

_____

_____

_____

Remember to bring the completed worksheet to your next appointment.

MEMORIES AND REMEMBRANCES

The five exercises in this section will help clients think about what it means to keep a memory and a relationship alive, and how to commemorate that relationship. This is another section that facilitates community building, as the exercises concentrate on expressing memories in an external way and often sharing them with others.

These exercises, and the general focus of the grief work in this and the remaining sections, are most appropriate for clients who have entered, or are nearing, the final stage of their grief work (reclamation and reconciliation).

As a reminder, Stage 2 tasks include the following:

- Contending with reality
- Developing insight
- Reconstructing values and beliefs
- Accepting changes and feelings and letting go

Stage 3 tasks include the following:

- Developing social relations
- Making decisions about lifestyle changes
- Renewing self-awareness
- Accepting responsibility for decisions and moving on

PURPOSE

The work in this section is primarily about helping clients understand how to keep memories fresh and find ways to express them so that they become an important part of both life and continued recovery from grief.

TYPES OF SITUATIONS FOR WHICH THIS INFORMATION MAY BE MOST USEFUL

Clients are not ready to work on exercises in this section unless they have worked through many of the issues and tasks of Stages 1 and 2. The exercises in this section are designed to help transform memories into fond nostalgia, rather than memories that sting and cause pain.

MEMORIES AND REMEMBRANCES

As you work toward containing, understanding, and expressing your sorrow, memories will continually pop and in out of your thoughts, shaping and affecting your feelings.

Just as the end of mourning isn't marked by the absence of feelings, it isn't marked by the end of memory, either. Neither would we want it to be. Memories are an important tool in your grief work—they help to keep your relationship alive, and help you deal with grief. As you move through your grief, you'll find that your memories are not only sad—perhaps overwhelmingly so, at first—but also increasingly nostalgic.

MEMORIES AND NOSTALGIA

It's true that memories can make you wince, make you sad, and remind you of the things you've lost. But they can also make you smile, provide comfort, and recall the best of times. Just as you use your grief work to express your thoughts and feelings, you can also use it to capture the memories that provide the warmth of nostalgia.

Memories keep the past alive, and link your present to your past. For some people, especially those who have experienced trauma, memories are difficult things to deal with. But for most people, memories serve to positively connect their present to their past. They allow us to remember lessons learned and to recall past pleasures of all kinds. Nostalgia has a special power. It allows us to look back in fondness and enjoy the past, even if we miss it and are homesick for it. It is through this fond recall that memories promote healing, allowing us to revisit the past and draw inspiration and courage to face the present. Nostalgia can bring the past to life, helping to make present difficulties more tolerable.

The loss of memory is one of the most crushing ailments imaginable, as it places us only in the present, leaving us stranded without the benefit of past wisdom, experience, and inspiration.

KEEPING MEMORY ALIVE

With the passing of your loved one, the living relationship you had ended. But this doesn't mean you no longer have a relationship, nor does it mean you shouldn't have one. Your relationship is kept alive through your memories, and the memories of others in your family and circle of friends. Memories of what you had together, and what you meant to one another. Recollections of your loved one and stories of his or her life—snapshots of the past that keep it close to you, and available whenever you choose to look back.

TELLING TALES

GOALS OF THE EXERCISE

This exercise has the client recall tales about the loved one and encourages the collecting, exchanging, and telling of them. It directs the client to talk to other people who were also close in some way to the deceased, and collect and document stories that keep memory alive. This sort of exercise not only expresses ideas, thoughts, and feelings but also builds a biographical record of the life of the deceased and the life of the client.

TYPES OF SITUATIONS FOR WHICH THIS EXERCISE MAY BE MOST USEFUL

The exercise is an appropriate way to start the process of exploring and reminiscing about the life of the deceased.

SUGGESTIONS FOR PROCESSING THIS EXERCISE WITH CLIENTS

- What was compiling this exercise like for you? Was it uncomfortable at first, or did it come easily and naturally?

- Was it easy or difficult to find stories to be told? Are there more stories to tell?

- Whose tale you did you tell for this exercise—your own or someone else's? Why did you make that choice?

- Will you share these stories with anyone else as you compile them?

TELLING TALES

For this exercise, think of fond memories—things or stories about your loved one that stand out in your mind and bring back good memories.

1. Besides yourself, who else has stories to tell—who else knows your loved one well enough to tell their own tales?

   _____

   _____

   _____

   _____

2. Talk to four of these people, and from each gather three stories. Who will you talk to?

   _____

   _____

   _____

   _____

3. For this exercise pick one tale to tell. Whose story is this?

   _____

4. Why did you pick this story for this exercise?

   _____

   _____

   _____

   _____

5. Had you heard this story before you gathered it for this exercise? What was it like to hear the story for the first time, or to hear or tell it again?

_____

_____

_____

_____

6. Tell the story.

_____

_____

_____

_____

_____

_____

_____

_____

_____

_____

_____

_____

_____

_____

_____

_____

_____

_____

_____

_____

_____

_____

_____

_____

7. What was it like to tell this tale?

_____

_____

_____

_____

8. How does telling this tale leave you feeling?

_____

_____

_____

_____

9. Is there anything you'd like to add to this story?

_____

_____

_____

_____

Remember to bring the completed worksheet to your next appointment.

A SCRAPBOOK

GOALS OF THE EXERCISE

This is a very focused exercise designed to help clients create and build a scrapbook memorializing the life of their loved one.

TYPES OF SITUATIONS FOR WHICH THIS EXERCISE MAY BE MOST USEFUL

This is an exercise for clients who want (or are willing) to create a book that collects and captures memorabilia of their loved one and his or her life. Memory books such as this can be very powerful, and the process (and the finished product) can be very important for any client—of any age—who wants to engage in this process of memorialization. The process and product often serve multiple purposes, including facilitating catharsis and symbolizing the ability to move on after the death.

SUGGESTIONS FOR PROCESSING THIS EXERCISE WITH CLIENTS

- Will your memory book be an ongoing work to which you continually add material, or will you stop after its initial creation? How will you know the right amount of memorabilia to include in your scrapbook?

- Is it comforting to create a memory book, or is it difficult at this time? Will the way you use a memory book change over time? Will the sort of memorabilia you add differ as you work through your grief, more fully reclaim your life, and move on?

- How often will you look through your memory book? Is there a risk that you will refer to it *too* often, and that it might hold you back in your ability to move on?

A SCRAPBOOK

1. What sort of memorabilia exists that can be easily gathered and placed in, or attached to, a memory book? Add ideas of your own.

   ____ Artwork   ____ Awards   ____ Certificates

   ____ Favorite poems   ____ Insignia   ____ Jewelry

   ____ Letters   ____ Music   ____ Newspaper clippings

   ____ Photographs   ____ Ticket stubs   ____ Writing

   _____

   _____

   _____

   _____

2. What other sort of things remind you of your loved one, but can't fit into a scrapbook?

   _____

   _____

   _____

   _____

3. Is there some way to creatively attach some of these other mementos, or make reference to them, so that they can be included in a memory book?

   _____

   _____

   _____

   _____

4. Are there things that you can create yourself—such as poems, drawings, or collages—
   that will help you remember certain aspects of your loved one, or certain days in your
   life together?

   _____

   _____

   _____

   _____

5. Are there things that you can collect from other people that can be included in your
   book of memories?

   _____

   _____

   _____

   _____

6. Write an introduction to your memory book that you can later add as the cover page.

   _____

   _____

   _____

   _____

Remember to bring the completed work sheet to your next appointment.

A TRIP IN TIME

GOALS OF THE EXERCISE

This exercise and the following one are linked. Each directs clients to think back into the past shared with their loved one, and describe people, places, and things from that shared history.

TYPES OF SITUATIONS FOR WHICH THIS EXERCISE MAY BE MOST USEFUL

This exercise will help clients bring memories into the present. Like many of the exercises, this is one intended to be used repeatedly.

SUGGESTIONS FOR PROCESSING THIS EXERCISE WITH CLIENTS

- What's it like to recollect this aspect of your shared past?
- Is there some reason you can't revisit this person, place, or thing?
- What might it be like to revisit? What does it feel like to even consider a visit?

A TRIP IN TIME

1. Name at least three people from your shared past with your loved one. These can be relatives, friends, old roommates, or school teachers—anyone who is still alive, but not in your current life. Name only people who evoke special memories of your relationship with your loved one.

_____

_____

_____

_____

_____

_____

2. Name at least three places from your shared past. These can include places you lived, places you visited frequently, and places you visited infrequently or only once. Name only places from your shared past that carry strong memories of your relationship.

_____

_____

_____

_____

_____

_____

3. Name at least three things you used to do together—not in your life immediately prior to the death, but from your past. Think about activities you used to share, like long walks, eating popcorn and watching an old movie, or watching the stars together at night. Once again, think about only those that have special memories of times spent together.

_____

_____

_____

_____

_____

_____

Pick one of these people, place, or things—the rest of this exercise will focus only on that choice. This is an exercise that you can repeat for each of the people, places, and things you've named above.

4. Who, where, or what have you chosen for the exercise?

_____

5. What special memories are attached?

_____

_____

_____

_____

_____

_____

Remember to bring the completed worksheet to your next appointment.

A VISIT THROUGH TIME

GOALS OF THE EXERCISE

Building on the previous exercise, this exercise has the client pay a visit to the person, place, or thing described. Again, the goal is keeping important memories alive—not through simple reminiscing, but through the active process of memorialization. On a note of caution, the idea is *not* to keep the client stuck in the past.

TYPES OF SITUATIONS FOR WHICH THIS EXERCISE MAY BE MOST USEFUL

Why simply reminisce when it's sometimes possible to revisit? As an example, high school reunions allow the past to come back to life, and transform memories into current experiences. Sometimes revisiting the past, and thus bringing it into the present, evokes new feelings, puts old memories into a more honest and clear light, refreshes memory, or serves as a turning point for new decisions or new relationships.

SUGGESTIONS FOR PROCESSING THIS EXERCISE WITH CLIENTS

- Will you consider visiting with this person, place, or thing again? Has this trip affected your plans to visit other people, places, or things?

- What was the best part about this visit? What was the most difficult part?

- Is there someone you can share these memories and experiences with? Who, and what will that be like? If not, why not?

A VISIT THROUGH TIME

In the previous homework exercise ("A Trip in Time"), you described people, places, and things connected to your loved one and your memories of your relationship. Now pay a visit to the person, place, or thing you've chosen. Ideally, make your visit in person, if this is possible.

If a direct visit isn't possible and you've chosen a person, make a phone call, write a letter, or find some other way to get in contact. If you've chosen a place or thing to revisit, but can't go in person, look at old photos or other mementos that allow vivid recollection.

1. Who, where, or what did you visit?

_____

_____

_____

_____

2. Describe your visit.

_____

_____

_____

_____

_____

_____

_____

_____

_____

_____

_____

_____

3. What memories did your visit bring back?

_____
_____
_____
_____
_____
_____

4. What feelings were evoked for you?

_____
_____
_____
_____

5. In what ways did your visit affect your sense of shared history or connect you to your loved one?

_____
_____
_____
_____

6. How did this visit to the past leave you feeling?

_____
_____
_____
_____

Remember to bring the completed worksheet to your next appointment.

COMMEMORATING YOUR LOVED ONE

GOALS OF THE EXERCISE

This exercise has clients think about the memorialization and commemoration of their loved one. It builds on a sense of community, as commemoration almost always means sharing with and connecting to others who also bereave the loss.

TYPES OF SITUATIONS FOR WHICH THIS EXERCISE MAY BE MOST USEFUL

This exercise will help clients consider whether they want to establish a commemoration, what it might be, and who might be affected.

For many, a simple act of commemoration may be adequate—the annual lighting of a candle or the periodic gathering of a group of people, for instance. For others, a far more structured and clear memorial is important—the donation of money, the naming of a building or object (it is not unusual, for example, to see a park bench named for someone who has passed on). Sometimes, those who have died needlessly at the hands of another or of an unjust society are memorialized in name through the changes their death has brought—Megan's Law, for instance.

The effort to make the loss *stand* for something is one way that people seek to find or recover meaning from an otherwise meaningless situation. Bereaved parents who build an organization to help others avoid a similar loss or assist those who have experienced the same loss are not only lending help to others, but also memorializing their own loss and giving *personal* meaning to the death—a reason to go on, and a foundation on which to build their own life and move on. Others may seek a different kind of meaning—a personal meaning that is more spiritual and inward, rather than directed outward to society as a whole.

SUGGESTIONS FOR PROCESSING THIS EXERCISE WITH CLIENTS

- Is it important to have more than one kind of commemoration? Do you need one commemoration for yourself alone, and another for others to share?

- Will you plan this memorial alone, or will you allow others to share in its design?

- How will this memorial or commemoration give meaning to your life?

COMMEMORATING YOUR LOVED ONE

1. I want a memorial to . . .

_____

_____

_____

_____

2. This commemoration will preserve . . .

_____

_____

_____

_____

3. This commemoration will celebrate . . .

_____

_____

_____

_____

4. What sort of commemoration or memorial might you plan—a building or physical monument, a gathering or event, a donation or expression of giving to others? Describe some of your ideas.

_____

_____

_____

_____

5. Who else will be directly affected by this memorial? Check off all the people who will be affected and moved by this commemoration, and add others not listed here. (Next to each, briefly write how they will be affected.)

_____ No one else will be affected

_____ Children: _____

_____ Parents: _____

_____ Siblings: _____

_____ In-laws: _____

_____ Friends: _____

_____ Colleagues: _____

_____ : _____

_____ : _____

_____ : _____

_____ : _____

6. What message do you most want this commemoration to give?

_____

_____

_____

_____

Remember to bring the completed worksheet to your next appointment.

Section XII

UNFINISHED BUSINESS

As clients move further through their grief work, they may reach a point where issues with the deceased or surrounding the death need to be expressed and, perhaps, expunged. The four exercises in this section focus the client on letting go of old, unfinished business that can never be resolved with the loved one, gathering up loose emotional ends, and beginning to find closure.

PURPOSE

The material covered in this section will assist clients in identifying, and perhaps being honest about, unresolved issues, feelings, and unfinished business in general.

TYPES OF SITUATIONS FOR WHICH THIS INFORMATION MAY BE MOST USEFUL

This aspect of grief work means working with clients to help them explore and understand what, if any, unfinished business requires closure.

UNFINISHED BUSINESS

With the passing of your loved one, you may have been left with the feeling that so much was left undone or unsaid—part of you may even feel incomplete because something has been left incomplete in your relationship. But, unlike other relationships that end, in the case of a death, there's no chance for reconciliation, no way to go back and resolve unsettled issues or wish one another the best. With the sad reality of a death, the relationship ends, suddenly and forever.

But this irrevocable end doesn't mean that there aren't things that need to be addressed, resolved, and put to rest. The difference is that you have to find a way to bring closure to the relationship on your own—here, the task is to come to terms with the uncompleted aspects of your relationship and move on.

UNFINISHED BUSINESS

The things you never did, and the things you could have done differently. The words you should have said, or the words you shouldn't have said. Those things you wanted to hear from your loved one but never did, or the words that were said but you wish were never spoken. The unresolved issues, differences, and feelings. The unfulfilled plans and expectations. This is the stuff of unfinished business. A bag full of feelings that are unfulfilled or left hanging—an incomplete situation.

Following your loss, you may have unfinished business with your loved one. You may feel angry, guilty, resentful, or regretful. But with the death of your loved one, there is no one to resolve issues with—except yourself. The task of resolution now becomes a personal one. This task is one that you must work through in your grief work, involving your ability to wrap up loose ends and find a way to bring closure to the situation.

TYING UP LOOSE ENDS

Tying up the loose ends means first identifying what those loose ends are—what business has been left incomplete. It also means recognizing that resolution is a state of mind, a perspective in which you are able to accept that which is unchangeable and through which you are able to explore and express feelings. In many ways, completing unfinished business is finding a way to say goodbye.

The tasks of completing unfinished business are self-expression, contemplation, and letting go. These are personal tasks; when you complete them, you will have changed nothing in the world around you, and you will have changed no one else. But as you resolve unfinished business, you change yourself.

THINKING ABOUT UNFINISHED BUSINESS

GOALS OF THE EXERCISE

Exercises like this one are not for everyone—not everyone has unfinished business with their deceased loved one. In this exercise, clients will begin to think about their unfinished business and reflect on what issues need to be stated and addressed, if any.

TYPES OF SITUATIONS FOR WHICH THIS EXERCISE MAY BE MOST USEFUL

This exercise will help clients decide whether they have unfinished business that needs resolution and, if so, the type and depth of resolution needed.

SUGGESTIONS FOR PROCESSING THIS EXERCISE WITH CLIENTS

- How important is closure for you? Why?

- What kind of help or support might you need to help address and resolve your unfinished business?

- How deeply experienced is your unfinished business?

- Who can you turn to when you need some encouragement, comfort, or words of wisdom?

THINKING ABOUT UNFINISHED BUSINESS

In this exercise, begin to think about the sort of unfinished business in your life. At this point, focus only on the broad issues you may have—don't worry about the details. Here, you're trying to look at your own thoughts and get in touch with your feelings, without focusing too deeply on the content and details of those thoughts or feelings.

The first question to ask yourself is, do you need closure on your relationship? Not everybody does. But even if you don't feel that you need deep closure or have much in the way of unfinished business, read through this exercise and complete as much of it as fits.

1. Is the kind of closure you need more like saying goodbye and expressing your simple sorrow, or is it more like trying to vent deep feelings that have been left unresolved?

   _____

   _____

   _____

   _____

2. What kinds of unfinished business do you have? (Check all that apply, and add other types of unfinished business that you may have.)

   ____ Unresolved feelings   ____ Unshared experiences

   ____ Unexpressed thoughts   ____ Unspoken words

   ____ Unstated regrets   ____ Untold secrets

   _____

   _____

   _____

   _____

3. Of the things you checked off or added, which are about you—your thoughts and feelings, your actions, or your words? Which are about your loved one—his or her feelings, actions, or words?

Unfinished business about my *actions, feelings, words, or thoughts*

_____

_____

_____

_____

Unfinished business about the actions, feelings, or words of my loved one

_____

_____

_____

_____

4. Are your main issues about things that were done—things that you or your loved one did or said, but perhaps shouldn't have? Or are they about things that were never done or said, but perhaps should have been?

_____

_____

_____

_____

5. Tying up loose ends can be difficult and painful. What part will be the hardest for you?

_____

_____

_____

_____

6. What most concerns you as you think about resolving unfinished business?

_____

_____

_____

_____

7. Do you need to complete unfinished business? If so, why?

_____

_____

_____

_____

Remember to bring the completed worksheet to your next appointment.

EXPRESSING YOUR FEELINGS

GOALS OF THE EXERCISE

This exercise opens with structured sentence starts to help clients get in touch with and express feelings. It concludes with a focus on only one of the feelings initially identified and expressed. This exercise can be used repeatedly to help clients begin the process of closing down and putting away unfinished business.

TYPES OF SITUATIONS FOR WHICH THIS EXERCISE MAY BE MOST USEFUL

This is a relatively structured exercise to help clients get in touch with unresolved feelings or expectations. The exercise should be used repeatedly to help clients recognize unresolved feelings or issues and address them briefly, thus providing material for deeper exploration in therapy or elsewhere.

SUGGESTIONS FOR PROCESSING THIS EXERCISE WITH CLIENTS

- Does thinking and writing about this issue help you better understand this piece of unfinished business?

- As you work on expressing your feelings, what other feelings are evoked for you? Do you feel guilty about your feelings, or do you feel a sense of relief?

- Does writing about this piece of unfinished business help get it off your mind? Do you need to revisit this piece of unfinished business again, in order to work on resolving your feelings about it?

EXPRESSING YOUR FEELINGS

1. Complete the sentence for each feeling that applies for you. Add other feelings you may be having and an explanation.

I feel . . .

Angry *because* . . .   _____

_____

Apologetic *because* . . .   _____

_____

Ashamed *because* . . .   _____

_____

Betrayed *because* . . .   _____

_____

Cheated *because* . . .   _____

_____

Crushed *because* . . .   _____

_____

Curious *because* . . .   _____

_____

Doubtful *because* . . .   _____

_____

Exploited *because* . . .   _____

_____

Guilty *because* . . .   _____

_____

_____

Hurt *because* . . . _____

Irritated *because* . . . _____

Mistreated *because* . . . _____

Offended *because* . . . _____

Regretful *because* . . . _____

Resentful *because* . . . _____

Vengeful *because* . . . _____

_____ *because* . . . _____

_____ *because* . . . _____

_____ *because* . . . _____

_____ *because* . . . _____

_____ *because* . . . _____

2. Take any one of these feelings or issues, and elaborate on it now. Which of these issues is most pressing for you right now?

_____

_____

_____

_____

3. What makes this unfinished business for you?

_____

_____

_____

_____

4. What about this issue is left undone?

_____

_____

_____

_____

5. What do you want to say to your loved one about this piece of unfinished business?

_____

_____

_____

_____

Remember to bring the completed worksheet to your next appointment.

REGRETS

GOALS OF THE EXERCISE

In this exercise, through a series of structured sentence starts, clients reflect on and express regrets and sorrows.

TYPES OF SITUATIONS FOR WHICH THIS EXERCISE MAY BE MOST USEFUL

This exercise will be helpful for clients who haven't been able to fully recognize or express feelings or regrets, or clients who are unable to let go of sorrows and unfinished business easily.

SUGGESTIONS FOR PROCESSING THIS EXERCISE WITH CLIENTS

- Are there things you can do about any of your unresolved regrets? Are there physical actions you can take in your life that might help you feel better about some of your regrets?

- What have you learned—or can you learn—about unresolved issues and regrets from this exercise?

- Are there other problem situations in your life right now with current relationships—things unsaid or undone—that you need to be aware of and correct before they later become unresolved regrets?

REGRETS

Addressing unfinished business doesn't necessarily require endless hours of soul searching, finding ways to resolve complex emotional issues. Sometimes, it requires no more than voicing regret for things done or things left undone.

Expressing regret isn't intended as a way to dwell on and wish away that which has past. Instead, quite simply, it's a way to express sorrow—and sometimes remorse—for missed opportunity, a way to exorcize and relieve yourself of an otherwise unspoken burden. Use this simple exercise to voice any previously unvoiced regrets.

I wish *I'd* said . . . _____

_____

_____

I wish *you'd* said . . . _____

_____

_____

I wish I had . . . _____

_____

_____

I wish I hadn't . . . _____

_____

_____

I wish you had . . . _____

_____

_____

I wish you hadn't . . . _____

_____

_____

I wish I could change . . . _____

_____

_____

I'm sorry for . . . _____

_____

_____

I wish . . . _____

_____

_____

_____

_____

I wish . . . _____

_____

_____

_____

_____

I wish . . . _____

_____

_____

_____

_____

Remember to bring the completed worksheet to your next appointment.

UNFINISHED BUSINESS

GOALS OF THE EXERCISE

Clients can use the final exercise in this section to think about how their lives are affected by unfinished business, and what they need to do to put closure on those unresolved issues and move on.

TYPES OF SITUATIONS FOR WHICH THIS EXERCISE MAY BE MOST USEFUL

The work of unfinished business is, often, never really complete; in reality, unfinished business frequently remains unfinished, a work continually in process. However, this exercise will help clients to assess their needs regarding unfinished business and wrap up loose ends.

SUGGESTIONS FOR PROCESSING THIS EXERCISE WITH CLIENTS

*   Do you have unfinished business with the *living?*

*   Are there homework exercises in this section that you should be repeating more than once?

*   Is it too difficult to resolve unfinished business on your own? Do you need to turn to anyone else in your support system—or outside your current support system—for help?

UNFINISHED BUSINESS

1. Are you ready to bring closure to unfinished business with your loved one, or do you still have business to finish up?

   _____

   _____

   _____

   _____

2. Has this work left you feeling unsettled?

   _____

   _____

   _____

   _____

3. Do you need to forgive your loved one?

   _____

   _____

   _____

   _____

4. Do you need to forgive yourself?

   _____

   _____

   _____

   _____

5. What will it take to finish unfinished business with your loved one?

_____

_____

_____

_____

6. Are you able to move on with your life? Are you ready to work toward reclamation and renewal, or do you feel you have more work to do with the tasks of this middle stage in your grief work?

_____

_____

_____

_____

Remember to bring the completed worksheet to your next appointment.

Section XIII

RELATIONSHIPS

By this section, the client should be well into or near the third stage of grief work, reclamation and reconciliation. Simply put, in this stage the issues involve moving on and fully building and living a life without the deceased. This section contains five exercises to help clients focus on current and new relationships.

PURPOSE

This section will help clients consider current and future relationships in their lives and understand the changing nature and role of relationships as they work through grief issues.

TYPES OF SITUATIONS FOR WHICH THIS INFORMATION MAY BE MOST USEFUL

This work is most appropriate for clients who are coming to terms with their relationships as they settle into their lives without their love one.

RELATIONSHIPS

One of the most significant aspects of life is social interaction—the personal relationships and community that connect you to other people.

Community is about shared values and experiences, but above all about an intimacy that exists between its members. As you move on with your life, it's important to think about, build on, and perhaps renew your current relationships—and, more than likely, build new relationships as well.

RECONFIGURING RELATIONSHIPS

There are many relationships in your life, and there will be many more to come. In many ways, we define ourselves by our relationships. How you see yourself is quite likely affected deeply by your relationships—the more positive, gratifying, and supportive relationships you've had, the more likely you are to feel good about yourself.

Most of the exercises in this workbook are about relationships—especially your relationship with your loved one. But as you move on with your life, the focus increasingly shifts to your relationships with others—those in your past, present, and future.

Under the best of circumstances, it can be difficult to deal with relationships. And making sense of relationships is undoubtedly one of the most complex tasks you'll face in your ongoing grief work. Obviously, there are many possible scenarios that revolve around changed needs, expectations, and desires in relationships of every kind. But, whatever the specifics, part of your task is to understand your relationships, how you feel about them, and how to ensure that your relationships are what they need to be and—whenever possible—what you want them to be.

CURRENT RELATIONSHIPS

GOALS OF THE EXERCISE

This initial exercise will help clients in considering how relationships are important to them and thinking about their current relationships, both satisfying and unsatisfying.

TYPES OF SITUATIONS FOR WHICH THIS EXERCISE MAY BE MOST USEFUL

This exercise is especially useful for helping to warm up clients to the process of examining and defining their relationships, taking an honest and clear look at what relationships— and what aspects of relationships—are satisfying and dissatisfying, and why.

SUGGESTIONS FOR PROCESSING THIS EXERCISE WITH CLIENTS

- Important relationships aren't necessarily satisfying relationships. Is there a difference between an important and a satisfying relationship?

- Are you generally satisfied by the relationships in your life at this time? If not, is it easy to be honest with yourself about relationships that dissatisfy?

- Are there some relationships in your life that may not satisfy you, but are nevertheless important or permanent relationships? If so, is there anything you can do to improve the quality of these so they meet more of your needs?

CURRENT RELATIONSHIPS

There is a different between *important* relationships and *satisfying* relationships. Some relationships are very important, yet unsatisfying. This exercise will help you examine your current relationships.

1. List five important relationships, and briefly describe why they're important.

Important Relationship

Important Because

_____

_____

_____

_____

_____

_____

_____

_____

_____

_____

2. Identify which current relationships are *satisfying,* and briefly describe why.

Satisfying Relationship

What Makes This Relationship Satisfying

_____

_____

_____

_____

_____

_____

---------------------------------   ---------------------------------

---------------------------------   ---------------------------------

---------------------------------   ---------------------------------

---------------------------------   ---------------------------------

---------------------------------   ---------------------------------

---------------------------------   ---------------------------------

---------------------------------   ---------------------------------

                                                  ----

3. Identify which current relationships are *unsatisfying*, and briefly describe why.

Unsatisfying Relationship   **What Makes This Relationship Unsatisfying**

_____   _____

_____   _____

                            _____

                            _____

_____   _____

                            _____

4. In general, what do seek from relationships? What makes a relationship satisfying to you?

_____

_____

_____

_____

5. What is it about a relationship that eventually makes it unsatisfying for you?

_____

_____

_____

_____

6. Are all of your _important_ relationships also _satisfying_ relationships?

_____

_____

_____

_____

7. What do you most want to change about any of your relationships in general?

_____

_____

_____

_____

Remember to bring the completed worksheet to your next appointment.

EVOLVING RELATIONSHIPS

GOALS OF THE EXERCISE

Some relationships will strengthen after the death of someone close, and some will weaken. This exercise will help clients think about how and why their relationships have changed since the death of the loved one.

TYPES OF SITUATIONS FOR WHICH THIS EXERCISE MAY BE MOST USEFUL

This exercise will help clients think about why some relationships have changed, and how they have changed. The exercise concludes by focusing on a single relationship, allowing clients to discuss what they really want from this particular relationship and why, as well as why (and how) the relationship has changed since the death of the loved one. In some cases, this may signal the end of a relationship that is no longer satisfying or the need for a major change. In other cases, a new relationship may be blossoming, or there may now be an opportunity for a new relationship to develop.

At this point in their grief work, clients may be ready to develop new relationships, or to take old relationships in new directions. Equally, it may be important for some clients to shift, or even end, existing relationships. Some of this work may be difficult, as it may be filled with fear, shame, or guilt. Nevertheless, at this stage in grief work, it is important for clients to tackle these issues as they truly move on with their lives. The exercise can, and should, be used repeatedly to explore different relationships.

SUGGESTIONS FOR PROCESSING THIS EXERCISE WITH CLIENTS

- Do you have the power to bring about change in this relationship now? If so, how can you do this? If not, what is impeding change?

- Do you feel capable of overcoming the impact of death of your relationships?

- Should your focus be on restoring current relationships, building new ones, or both?

- Does this exercise raise difficult feelings for you—perhaps sadness or more loss, or feelings of shame or guilt?

- Are you at a point where you see and feel a need for a new relationship, or the development of an existing relationship in a new direction? If so, what feelings does that raise?

EVOLVING RELATIONSHIPS

1. My relationships have most changed because . . .

_____

_____

_____

_____

2. The way that my relationships have changed since the death is . . .

_____

_____

_____

_____

3. The relationships that have been affected the most are . . .

_____

_____

_____

_____

4. Some relationships may have been strengthened in some way since your loss, and others in some way weakened. Think about your relationships, and why they've changed.

Strengthened Relationship   **Changed in What Way?**

_____   _____

                                       _____

_____   _____

                                       _____

_____   _____

_____   _____

_____   _____

_____   _____

_____   _____

_____   _____

_____   _____

_____   _____

_____   _____

_____   _____

Weakened Relationship   **Changed in What Way?**

_____   _____

_____   _____

_____   _____

_____   _____

_____   _____

_____   _____

_____   _____

_____   _____

_____   _____

_____   _____

_____   _____

_____   _____

_____   _____

_____   _____

5. Pick one of these relationships, and describe it further. You can repeat the exercise for each relationship, if you choose.

   Relationship:

   This relationship has changed because . . .

   _____

   _____

   _____

   The impact of the death on this relationship has been . . .

   _____

   _____

   _____

   What I want most from this relationship is . . .

   _____

   _____

   _____

   _____

Remember to bring the completed worksheet to your next appointment.

REMAKING RELATIONSHIPS

GOALS OF THE EXERCISE

Building on the previous exercises, this exercise focuses on a single relationship and on desired change—in any direction.

TYPES OF SITUATIONS FOR WHICH THIS EXERCISE MAY BE MOST USEFUL

This exercise provides a structured way to think about the shape of current relationships.

Again, this exercise can and should be used repeatedly to think about multiple relationships, one at a time.

SUGGESTIONS FOR PROCESSING THIS EXERCISE WITH CLIENTS

- It can be emotionally difficult to explore relationship issues—have you been honest with yourself as you've been working on these exercises? How have you dealt with any difficult emotions that may have come up for you?

- Do you feel like you have to make changes of any kind in your relationships? If so, how will you tackle them? Do you have anyone you can talk to about some of these changes?

REMAKING RELATIONSHIPS

Think about the relationships you've explored in previous homework exercises. Select an existing relationship that you want to change in some way.

1. Relationship with:
2. What sort of change are you looking for? (Check all that apply.)

   ____ Improvement   ____ Change the relationship in some way

   ____ Move in new direction   ____ Get closer

   ____ Gain distance from the relationship   ____ End the relationship

   Other: _____

3. What's motivating your desire to change this relationship?

   _____

   _____

   _____

   _____

4. Describe the change you want in more detail.

   _____

   _____

   _____

   _____

5. In what ways doesn't this relationship meet your present needs?

   _____

   _____

   _____

   _____

6. What do you think the other person wants or needs from this relationship?

_____

_____

_____

_____

7. How will changes affect the other person in this relationship?

_____

_____

_____

_____

8. If this is a relationship that can't be changed, what can you do to improve the situation for yourself?

_____

_____

_____

_____

9. What sorts of things stand in the way of making the changes you want?

_____

_____

_____

_____

Remember to bring the completed worksheet to your next appointment.

MOVING ON

GOALS OF THE EXERCISE

This exercise poses questions about new relationships and the client's motivations, hopes, and obstacles regarding them. Like many of the other exercises, this one concludes by reflecting on one relationship in particular.

TYPES OF SITUATIONS FOR WHICH THIS EXERCISE MAY BE MOST USEFUL

Not every client will be building, or wanting to build, new relationships. This exercise is intended for clients who are working on new relationships, or the idea of new relationships.

SUGGESTIONS FOR PROCESSING THIS EXERCISE WITH CLIENTS

- There are many kinds of relationships. When you think about new relationships, what comes to mind?
- Are others in your circle ready for you to build new relationships? How will you deal with resistance from friends or family members who may judge you or disapprove of new relationships?

MOVING ON

1. Are you ready for new relationships?

_____

_____

_____

_____

2. What new relationships do you want to build?

_____

_____

_____

_____

3. Why are you seeking a new relationship? What's the motivation?

_____

_____

_____

_____

4. Do you feel conflicted about the possibility of a new relationship?

_____

_____

_____

_____

5. Describe your feelings about seeking or having a new relationship.

_____

_____

_____

_____

6. What are your hopes for new relationships?

_____

_____

_____

_____

7. What's stopping you from seeking or getting involved in a new relationship?

_____

_____

_____

_____

8. What are your fears about a new relationship?

_____

_____

_____

_____

9. Is there a new relationship in particular that comes to mind? If so, write a little about that relationship now.

_____

_____

_____

_____

Remember to bring the completed worksheet to your next appointment.

CHECKPOINT: RELATIONSHIPS

GOALS OF THE EXERCISE

This final exercise helps clients take a general and summary look back at their relationships and reflect on what relationship work is still ahead.

TYPES OF SITUATIONS FOR WHICH THIS EXERCISE MAY BE MOST USEFUL

This exercise is designed for reviewing and briefly exploring relationship issues before either moving onto the final section or returning to more homework exercises within this section or in earlier sections.

SUGGESTIONS FOR PROCESSING THIS EXERCISE WITH CLIENTS

* New situations often accompany new relationships. Have you thought about new situations in your life? Are you ready for such changes?

* If you're having difficulties knowing what to do or how to deal with changing or new relationships, can you talk to someone? Who? How much will you share?

CHECKPOINT: RELATIONSHIPS

1. Do you have any issues with the way you're being treated by others who are sharing your loss?

   _____

   _____

   _____

   _____

2. If it applies, how well are you dealing with new relationships that others in your life may be making?

   _____

   _____

   _____

   _____

3. Is it important for you to talk directly to other people in your circle about your relationships or theirs?

   _____

   _____

   _____

   _____

4. As you complete the homework exercises in this section, how are you feeling about your relationships or the relationships of others?

   _____

   _____

   _____

   _____

5. Are there unaddressed relationship issues still hanging for you?

_____

_____

_____

_____

Remember to bring the completed worksheet to your next appointment.

Section XIV

MOVING ON

This is the final section, and the five exercises in this section are designed for those at the tail end of their active grief work, as they near the completion of Stage 3. This section will help those nearing the end of their grief work think about where to now, and how to get there.

PURPOSE

This section is designed to set the pace for completing formal grief work, helping clients to move out of an active grief-work mode and back into the normal flow of daily life and relationships, where grief and loss fall into the background, although perhaps ever present.

TYPES OF SITUATIONS FOR WHICH THIS INFORMATION MAY BE MOST USEFUL

This section focuses on completing the formal process of grief work. Clients should not be working on the exercises in this section if grief is still actively interfering with their daily lives.

MOVING ON

Moving on in your grief work doesn't mean moving away from feelings and memories. But it does mean that you're at a point in your life and grief work where you've fallen back into a daily routine of some kind, and most people expect you to be pretty much over your grief. It's not that anyone expects you to not still have strong feelings about your loss, but you're certainly expected to be able to return to some version of your life before the death of your loved one. In other words, although you're not *over* your loss—and may never be—you've fallen back into the day-to-day patterns of an everyday life, and are able to function much as anyone else.

This is a reasonable expectation. By now, your grief work should have taken you through many of the steps required to be able to function well once again, and by now you should be prepared to think about the rest of your life, rather than those parts that are in the past.

DECISIONS, DECISIONS, DECISIONS

GOALS OF THE EXERCISE

Clients will think and write about the sort of decisions they currently face and why, what opportunities for change are available, and what prevents them from making desired changes.

TYPES OF SITUATIONS FOR WHICH THIS EXERCISE MAY BE MOST USEFUL

This exercise provides a general overview of current life choices and decisions that clients face, including the opportunity for change. The exercise can help clients decide they want to move on, and plan how to do so.

SUGGESTIONS FOR PROCESSING THIS EXERCISE WITH CLIENTS

- Are the sorts of life decisions that you face now the result of your loss, or are they typical of the sorts of decisions you faced before the death of your loved one?

- Are the sorts of difficulties you currently face in making choices connected to your loss, or are they typical of decision-making difficulties you faced even before the death of your loved one?

- Are the circumstances of your life now inhibiting your ability to make changes, or do you need to change your general approach to decision making?

DECISIONS, DECISIONS, DECISIONS

1. Think about current decisions and choices in your life. What sorts of decisions are the hardest to make?

   _____

   _____

   _____

   _____

2. In what way has the death of your loved one led to the sorts of choices you're currently facing?

   _____

   _____

   _____

   _____

3. In what ways has the death of your loved one opened up your life to the possibility of change?

   _____

   _____

   _____

   _____

4. What sorts of opportunities for change exist in your life right now?

   _____

   _____

   _____

   _____

5. What sorts of changes would you generally like to make?

_____

_____

_____

_____

6. In general, what sorts of things in your current life force or limit your ability to make decisions?

_____

_____

_____

_____

7. What stops you from making changes?

_____

_____

_____

_____

8. How can you best move ahead with the changes you'd like to make?

_____

_____

_____

_____

Remember to bring the completed worksheet to your next appointment.

MAKING DECISIONS

GOALS OF THE EXERCISE

This exercise focuses entirely on one decision situation and provides a structured brainstorming format to think through and resolve the decision.

TYPES OF SITUATIONS FOR WHICH THIS EXERCISE MAY BE MOST USEFUL

The exercise is intended to help clients think through and resolve potentially difficult life choices, with a focus on the impact and consequences of chosen decisions.

The exercise should be used to think through and process different decisions, and can also be used to process different solutions to the same problem.

SUGGESTIONS FOR PROCESSING THIS EXERCISE WITH CLIENTS

- Has this exercise helped you to better understand the issues and choices involved in this decision?

- What stops you from making a choice and acting on it in this case?

- Can you afford to take a chance on this decision, or are the consequences irreversible?

- Are you giving this decision too little thought (being impetuous) or too much thought (being indecisive)?

MAKING DECISIONS

1. Briefly describe one situation or problem that you're currently trying to resolve.

   _____

   _____

2. What sort of solution choices do you have to resolve this issue. Name at least eight different decision choices.

   _____

   _____

   _____

   _____

   _____

   _____

   _____

   _____

   _____

   _____

3. Review the possible choices you've just identified, and select the four most rational and realistic choices. Under each, describe how this choice could fit the circumstances and reality of your life.

   • _Your choice:_ _____

      This solution fits because . . . _____

      _____

      _____

- *Your choice:* _____

  This solution fits because . . . _____

  _____

  _____

- *Your choice:* _____

  This solution fits because . . . _____

  _____

  _____

- *Your choice:* _____

  This solution fits because . . . _____

  _____

  _____

4. Now, select just one of these choices, and use it as the focal point for the remainder of this exercise. You might want to repeat this exercise several times in order to think through each of the possible choices you identified.

   Your choice: _____

5. Think about the possible consequences of this choice. Is there a price to pay, and if so, what is it?

   _____

   _____

   _____

   _____

6. If you make this choice, what sort of challenges and obstacles will you have to overcome to make this decision happen?

   _____

   _____

   _____

   _____

7. If you make this choice, what will you have to do to make it a reality?

_____

_____

_____

_____

8. How will your life be affected by this choice?

_____

_____

_____

_____

9. Is there anyone else whose life will be affected by this decision? If so, who, why, and how?

_____

_____

_____

_____

10. Is this a good solution?

_____

_____

_____

_____

11. Is this a solution you want to choose?

_____

_____

_____

_____

Remember to bring the completed worksheet to your next appointment.

IF ONLY YOU KNEW WHAT'S INSIDE OF ME NOW

GOALS OF THE EXERCISE

This is an open-ended exercise in the form of a letter to the world. The format provides three basic sentence starts and leaves it to the now-experienced client to write feelings. This exercise and the following one emphasize the expression of feelings through words.

TYPES OF SITUATIONS FOR WHICH THIS EXERCISE MAY BE MOST USEFUL

This exercise and those in the remainder of this section are intended for clients who feel released from their grief work and ready to move on with other aspects of their life and therapy. The exercise provides a method for both reflection and catharsis.

SUGGESTIONS FOR PROCESSING THIS EXERCISE WITH CLIENTS

- Are there other ways you need to publicly acknowledge your experiences or share them with others?

- Is there still more you need to say about your loss?

- Have you considered sharing some of your experiences, and sharing the stories that others have to tell, through a grief support group?

IF ONLY YOU KNEW WHAT'S INSIDE OF ME NOW

As you move farther into your life, what seems left undone? By now you've had the chance to think about and express your loss, to explore life after and since the death of your loved one, and to consider where to go now. What's been left undone or unsaid? You may have written an obituary, and you may have found a suitable way to commemorate and memorialize your loss. But even so, as you near the end of your grief work, it's important to provide a way to wrap up this part of your journey and bring closure to it.

For all you've said and written already, what last words are there, and what final goodbyes? What do you want to tell others about how you're feeling *now* about what you've been through on your healing journey, and how it's affected you?

This is a letter to the world.

Day: _____ Date: _____

I want you to know that . . .

_____

_____

_____

_____

If you knew what was inside of me now, you'd know . . .

_____

_____

_____

_____

My grief journey has left me feeling . . .

_____

_____

_____

_____

As I near the completion of my grief work . . .

_____

_____

_____

_____

Remember to bring the completed worksheet to your next appointment.

A GOODBYE LETTER

GOALS OF THE EXERCISE

Here the form of the exercise is a letter to the deceased. Like the previous exercise, it provides little structure other than sentence starts.

TYPES OF SITUATIONS FOR WHICH THIS EXERCISE MAY BE MOST USEFUL

Like the previous exercise, this exercise is intended for clients ready to move on and symbolically say goodbye to both their loved one and their grief work.

SUGGESTIONS FOR PROCESSING THIS EXERCISE WITH CLIENTS

• Reread your letter. Does it feel satisfying? Did you say what you wanted to? Is there more you want to say? Will you write another letter?

• Are you ready to say goodbye? Do you want to return to this homework exercise at a later time and rewrite your letter?

A GOODBYE LETTER

In the end, closure means just that—putting an final face on something, whether it be a time in your life, a place left behind, or a relationship. Closure means completing the missing part of the circle and finding a way to feel complete, as you move on and leave that part of your life behind.

Little in life is more final than saying goodbye. Here, though, you're not saying goodbye to your memories, your connection, or your ability to revisit your loved one many times over in many different ways. You're not even saying goodbye to your ability and right to keep talking to your loved one, or your desire to keep your relationship alive and important in its own way.

What you *are* doing is saying goodbye to those parts of the relationship that have ended and cannot be revisited, except in memory. Saying goodbye is a way of recognizing that there are some questions that can't be answered and some things that can't be said. The very act of saying goodbye is a way to finish unfinished business. In the next journal entry, write a farewell letter to your loved one. Although you can always write another letter at a later time, don't complete this entry until you're ready to say goodbye and let go of your unfinished business.

Date: _____

To: _____

I will always remember . . .

_____

_____

_____

_____

Before you left, I wish . . .

_____

_____

_____

_____

Your death left me feeling . . .

_____

_____

_____

_____

I want you to know that . . .

_____

_____

_____

_____

Now finish your letter. Write it free form—say anything you want to.

_____

_____

_____

_____

_____

_____

_____

_____

_____

_____

_____

_____

_____

Remember to bring the completed worksheet to your next appointment.

I'VE LEARNED . . .

GOALS OF THE EXERCISE

This final exercise, using sentence starts, allows clients to reflect back on what they've learned—about themselves, about others, and about grief itself—through their grief work and homework writing.

TYPES OF SITUATIONS FOR WHICH THIS EXERCISE MAY BE MOST USEFUL

This exercise will help clients look back at their grief-work process and consider their growth and gains, as well as the changes sparked in them by their loss. It will help clients wrap up and consolidate their own growth as they near or complete this formal process of grief work.

This work can just as easily be considered the end of one journey and the beginning of another. As grief work ends, clients are ready to engage in more growth, built on the lessons taught and learned through the grieving process and their grief work.

SUGGESTIONS FOR PROCESSING THIS EXERCISE WITH CLIENTS

- Was this a difficult exercise to complete? If it was, what made it difficult? Was it an important exercise?

- Can you honestly say you've learned something from your loss? If you can, do you know what it is you've learned?

- Have you grown as a person because of your grief? In what ways?

- In what ways are you ready to move on? Are there other areas of personal growth and effectiveness sparked by your grief work that are important to work on?

I'VE LEARNED . . .

As you put this part of your life behind you—not your loved one or the memories of your relationship, of course, but your *grief*—it's time to look ahead. What do you see? As you peer into the future, you may find that looking into the past helps.

> *Going on means going far.*
> *Going far means returning.*
> —LAO TSU

What have you gained from the sad experience of loss? In what ways have you grown as an individual, and what have you learned from your grief?

From my grief, I've learned . . . _____

_____

_____

_____

_____

I'm not the same person as I was because . . . _____

_____

_____

_____

_____

My greatest lesson has been . . . _____

_____

_____

_____

_____

About myself, I've learned . . . _____

_____

_____

_____

_____

About others, I've learned . . . _____

_____

_____

_____

_____

From my grief, I . . . _____ _____

_____

_____

_____

_____

Remember to bring the completed worksheet to your next appointment.

BIBLIOGRAPHY

Atig, T. (1996). *How We Grieve: Relearning the World.* New York: Oxford University Press.

Caplan, C., and G. Lang. (1995). *Grief's Courageous Journey.* Oakland, CA: New Harbinger.

Childs-Gowell, E. (1992). *Good Grief Rituals: Tools for Healing.* Barrytown, NY: Station Hill Press.

Kubler-Ross, E. (1969). *On Death and Dying.* New York: Collins.

Moller, D. W. (1996). *Confronting Death.* New York: Oxford University Press.

Rando, T. A. (1991). *How to Go on Living When Someone You Love Dies.* New York: Bantam.

Rich, P. (1999). *The Healing Journey through Grief: Your Journal for Reflection and Recovery.* New York: John Wiley & Sons.

Sanders, C. M. (1989). *Grief: The Mourning After.* New York: John Wiley & Sons.

Staudacher, C. (1987). *Beyond Grief: A Guide for Recovering from the Death of a Loved One.* Oakland, CA: New Harbinger.

ABOUT THE CD-ROM

INTRODUCTION

This appendix provides you with information on the contents of the CD that accompanies this book. For the latest and greatest information, please refer to the ReadMe file located at the root of the CD.

SYSTEM REQUIREMENTS

- A computer with a processor running at 120 Mhz or faster
- At least 32 MB of total RAM installed on your computer; for best performance, we recommend at least 64 MB
- A CD-ROM drive

Note: Many popular word processing programs are capable of reading Microsoft Word files. However, users should be aware that a slight amount of formatting might be lost when using a program other than Microsoft Word.

USING THE CD WITH WINDOWS

To install the items from the CD to your hard drive, follow these steps:

1. Insert the CD into your computer's CD-ROM drive.
2. The CD-ROM interface will appear. The interface provides a simple point-and-click way to explore the contents of the CD.

If the opening screen of the CD-ROM does not appear automatically, follow these steps to access the CD:

1. Click the Start button on the left end of the taskbar and then choose Run from the menu that pops up.
2. In the dialog box that appears, type **d:\setup.exe.** (If your CD-ROM drive is not drive d, fill in the appropriate letter in place of *d*.) This brings up the CD interface described in the preceding set of steps.

USING THE CD WITH A MAC

1. Insert the CD into your computer's CD-ROM drive.
2. The CD-ROM icon appears on your desktop, double-click the icon.
3. Double-click the Start icon.
4. The CD-ROM interface will appear. The interface provides a simple point-and-click way to explore the contents of the CD.

WHAT'S ON THE CD

The following sections provide a summary of the software and other materials you'll find on the CD.

Content

Includes all 82 homework assignments from the book in Word format. Homework assignments can be customized, printed out, and distributed to parent and child clients in an effort to extend the therapeutic process outside of the office. All documentation is included in the folder named "Content."

Applications

The following applications are on the CD:

Microsoft Word Viewer
Windows only. Microsoft Word Viewer is a freeware viewer that allows you to view, but not edit, most Microsoft Word files. Certain features of Microsoft Word documents may not display as expected from within Word Viewer.

USER ASSISTANCE

If you have trouble with the CD-ROM, please call the Wiley Product Technical Support phone number at (800) 762-2974. Outside the United States, call 1(317) 572-3994. You can also contact Wiley Product Technical Support at **http://support.wiley.com.** John Wiley & Sons will provide technical support only for installation and other general quality control items. For technical support of the applications themselves, consult the program's vendor or author.

   To place additional orders or to request information about other Wiley products, please call (800) 225-5945.

For information about the CD-ROM see pages 239–240.

WILEY
Publishers Since 1807